John Foley © Agence Opale

Jean Hatzfeld, an international reporter for *Libération* since 1973, is the author of many books, including *Machete Season: The Killers in Rwanda Speak* and *Life Laid Bare: The Survivors in Rwanda Speak*. He lives in Paris.

Linda Coverdale has translated more than forty books, including Jean Hatzfeld's previous books on Rwanda. Her translation of *Machete Season* won the 2006 Scott Moncrieff Prize. She lives in Brooklyn, New York.

ALSO BY JEAN HATZFELD

Machete Season: The Killers in Rwanda Speak
Life Laid Bare: The Survivors in Rwanda Speak

THE ANTELOPE'S STRATEGY

THE ANTELOPE'S STRATEGY

LIVING IN RWANDA AFTER THE GENOCIDE

A REPORT BY
JEAN HATZFELD

TRANSLATED FROM THE FRENCH BY
LINDA COVERDALE

PICADOR

———

FARRAR, STRAUS AND GIROUX · NEW YORK

CONTENTS

Maps appear on pages 29 and 39

THE ANTELOPE'S STRATEGY

MORE QUESTIONS?

"When Satan offered the seven deadly sins to mankind, the African took gluttony and anger. I don't know whether he was the first to choose or the last. I don't know what the Whites or Asians snagged for themselves, either, because I haven't traveled through this world. But I do know that our choice will always work against us. Greed sows more strife and warfare across Africa than drought or ignorance. And in the mayhem, it managed to sow our thousand hills with genocide."

Pausing with a slow smile, as if to soften her words, Claudine Kayitesi adds, "I am content to be African, for otherwise I could not be content with anything. But proud—no. Can one be proud while feeling troubled? I am simply proud to be Tutsi, yes, absolutely, because the Tutsis were supposed to have disappeared from this earth and I am definitely still here."

When I had last visited Nyamata, Claudine had been living in a house that had once belonged to a female cousin, where she was caring for a swarm of local kids whom she had helped to rescue after their parents had been murdered in the genocide. Perched at the top of a steep path on the hill of Rugarama, the adobe house had deeply fissured walls and a rusty sheet-metal roof, but it nestled in a magnificent, sweet-smelling garden tended by Claudine's own hands. At the far end of the yard stood a shed for cooking pots and a pen for the calf.

In 2003, however, when the farmers who own the neighboring fields were released from the Rilima penitentiary, Claudine became anxious. One of the farmers was the murderer of her sister, and she feared coming face to face with him at night. She was therefore relieved to move to another plot of land with her new husband, Jean-Damascène, a former primary-school classmate, after a memorable wedding she describes like this:

"My husband and I, we met again two years ago. We exchanged friendly words to begin with, we saw each other in a new light at the New Year, we agreed on things in July. The wedding was a splendid affair: the singers led up to the ceremony robed in colorful *pagnes*, just as in photographs; I wore the three traditional dresses, and my husband's hands were formal in white gloves. The church offered us its courtyard and its tablecloths. Three vans carried the wedding party—with Fanta sodas, sorghum wine, and Primus beer, of course. The revelry lasted some three unbelievable days. Thanks to the wedding, time wears a kind face at present, but only at present. Because I see clearly that the future has already been eaten up by what I lived through."

Today, Claudine lives in a new house, one of dozens of identical houses in a *mudugudu** on a rocky, brush-covered slope just above Nyamata's main road, a few kilometers from Kanzenze. When we arrive, she places a spray of artificial blossoms on the low table

---

* *After the genocide, the Rwandan government launched a nationwide project of emergency communal housing to replace the countless homes destroyed during the war (most of them Tutsi) and to give better security to rural families who had been scattered in forests and the bush. A* mudugudu *is a cluster of standard houses, sometimes with as many as three thousand units, some with only a few dozen. The houses are of fired brick, concrete, or adobe, with or without window frames, and roofed in corrugated metal.*

in the main room to set off the bouquets of real flowers, shoos a gang of curious kids from the courtyard, draws the curtains, and with a look of amusement sits down in one of the wooden armchairs.

"More questions?" she says in feigned astonishment. "Still about the killings. So you just can't stop. Why keep on? Why ask me? A person can feel uneasy, answering—and at fault from the very first line in the book. In the marshes, Tutsis lived like wild pigs. Drinking the blackish swamp water, grubbing on all fours for food in the night, relieving themselves in a frantic hurry. Worse, they lived as prey, as they told you, crawling in the slime, their ears pricked, waiting for the hunters' machetes. It was an unnatural hunt, because all this prey was meant to disappear without even being eaten. In a way, they experienced the battle between good and evil right before their eyes, stark and simple, so to speak.

"Myself, I would naturally think that good finally won out, since it gave me the chance to run away and survive, and now I'm well provided for. But the mama, papa, little sisters, and all the dying who whispered in the mud and who had no ears listening tenderly for their last words—they can't answer your questions anymore. All those chopped-up people who longed for a human breath of comfort, all those who knew they were leaving this earth bare naked because they'd been robbed of their clothes before the end, all the dead moldering away under the papyrus or drying up out in the sun—they've got no way to tell anyone they disagree."

Claudine has a painful secret, but she never complains of anything. Every morning she goes down with her husband to their field. At noon she lights the fire under the cooking pot. Afternoons she goes here and there, visiting her girlfriends, the church compound, Nyamata. She no longer demands reparations, and she has given up on justice. She avoids working with others, disdains all pretense, is not afraid to speak her mind. She makes no effort to hide her fears, her hatred of the killers, her envy of survivors who still have parents to welcome their grandchildren, or her frustration at having missed out on getting a nursing degree. In short, she says, "In difficult encounters I match evil looks with a straight-ahead stare"—evil looks that are in striking contrast to her cheerful face, her scarlet dresses, and the boisterousness of her two offspring, who are in constant orbit around her.

Grinning, she anticipates my question: "Yes, this calm is real. I have lovely children, a decently fertile field, a nice husband to help me along. A few years ago, after the killings, when you met me for the first time, I was a simple girl among scattered children, bereft of everything but drudgery and bad thoughts. And since then, this husband has turned me into a family lady in an unbelievable way. Courage tugs me by the hand every morning, even when I awaken from terrible dreams, or during the dry season. Life offers me its smiles, and I owe it my gratitude for not having abandoned me in the marshes.

"But for me, the chance to become someone is over. You will never hear answers from the real Claudine in response to your questions—because I'm no longer truly happy in my own skin. I've known the defilement of a bestial existence, I've witnessed the ferocity of the hyena and even worse—since animals are never that wicked. I was called a cockroach, as you know. I was raped by a savage creature. I was swept away to that place, out there, which no words of ours can ever match. But the worst walks on ahead of me. My heart will always look around suspiciously; I know so well now that destiny can break its simple promises.

"Good fortune has offered me a second life, and I won't push it away. But it will be half a life, because of the complete break. I was hunted by death, and I wanted to survive at any cost. Then, when I asked only to escape this world and the shame corroding my soul, I was plagued by fate.

"When I was a girl, I placed my trust in life with all my heart. Life betrayed me. To be betrayed by your neighbors, by the authorities, by the Whites—that is a staggering blow. It can make one behave badly. For example, a man turns to drink and refuses to take up the hoe, or a woman neglects her little ones and won't take care of herself anymore.

"But to be betrayed by life . . . who can bear that? It's too much. You lose all sense of where the right direction lies. Reason why, in the future, I will always stay one step to the side."

A LONG LINE OF HALLELUJAHS

In the dry season, a dusty yet dazzling torpor immobilizes Ri-lima, the most arid place in the Bugesera, a region of hills and marshes lying south of Kigali. High atop a butte rise the brick walls of the penitentiary. Although it is early in January, the prisoners crowded into the courtyard seem indifferent to the oppressive heat and can hardly contain themselves when the immense gates swing open before them. In their motley assortment of ragged clothes, the detainees surge forward in hurried little steps, as if eager to get out as fast as possible without any disorderly jostling.

Herded along by indifferent soldiers, they gather in the shade of a eucalyptus grove, the sole small island of green available to the personnel of the fortress. These men do not sing, unlike other prisoners in pink uniforms a little way off, who come and go without a glance in their direction, in two impeccable lines, hauling water from the lake. The whispers of the waiting men cannot conceal their excitement. Both feverish and docile, anxious and delighted, they don't seem to know what attitude to take, and understandably: to the amazement of everyone and especially themselves, they have just been released without any explanation, after seven years in prison.

Three weeks earlier, the news had come over the radio in a

laconic presidential bulletin delivered with all the brio of a weather report: an initial group of forty thousand prisoners, killers who had confessed to genocide, been convicted and jailed, would be released from six penitentiaries all across the country.

At the blast of a whistle, the men pass through the gates of Rilima, nodding obsequiously to the guards, and rush down a rocky slope, leaping over clumps of brush. Among them, together again, are most of the guys in the Kibungo Hill gang, the ones whom I interviewed and described in *Machete Season: The Killers in Rwanda Speak*. Pio Mutungirehe, the youngest farmer in the bunch (he was twenty in 1994), not so young anymore; Fulgence Bunani, thirteen years older, the eternal volunteer deacon, who has miraculously held on to his white sandals throughout his captivity; Jean-Baptiste Murangira, former civil servant, now ramrod straight in his role as the president of an association of repentant killers; Alphonse Hitiyaremye, who can't stop smiling and waving to the guards, his pals, anyone around him; Pancrace Hakizamungili, more cautious, almost suspicious, but already thinking about his first Primus beer; and Adalbert Munzigura, bursting with energy at the head of the parade, just as he was always out in front on the killing expeditions.

Pancrace remembers that last day in the penitentiary: "Really, I did not believe that we'd have a stroke of luck like that—getting out of prison someday. We certainly heard rumors from visitors, but I couldn't understand how they could be true. On January 2, 2003, when the radio read us the presidential communiqué, we were overcome with joy, which poured so fast from our lips we could exchange only simple encouraging words. And we spent our last night in song. Many prisoners didn't even want to eat anything. Two moods contended in the prison: those who had confessed sang hallelujah, and those who hadn't owned up yelled insults and words of frustration."

. . .

Pancrace's old pal Ignace Rukiramacumu describes his journey home: "I thought about the *urwagwa** we would drink. I'd been convinced that we would never again taste it in this life, that they had shut the door behind us until the end of the world. Before that liberation, each time a violent epidemic attacked us, we'd imagined we would soon lie buried in prison. We used to count the number of dead, the number left behind, and calculate how long we would last.

"Because of my great age,† I rode in a truck reserved for the old and the sick. We stopped in Nyamata, when it was dark. That first night, we didn't dare go directly up through the forest; we huddled in the courtyard of the district office building. In the morning we shouldered our bags. It was a market day. Twice we walked around, afraid to approach, before beginning the climb up the paths. Among the people we met coming down to market, we recognized some survivors. I heard shouts of outrage as we went along, threats of vengeance, but that didn't last. Some folks called out greetings, even though you could hear they weren't kindly meant."

The youngest of the gang—Pio, Pancrace, Fulgence, Alphonse—left Rilima on foot, as Alphonse recalls: "We were a line of two thousand prisoners. Walking along, we heard friendly words as well as mockery and malicious remarks—reason why we hushed

---

* Urwagwa, *banana beer*—three times cheaper and three times more potent than ordinary beer—can be delicious. Bananas are buried for several days in a pit; then their juice is pressed out and mixed with sorghum flour, left several more days to ferment, strained, and bottled. Urwagwa varies in strength, tartness, and "bite," depending on the time of year and the brewer's expertise, and it must be drunk within a few days. The buyer passes around the bottle, with a single reed straw, to his drinking companions. Hutus brew the best urwagwa, but Tutsis prove their equals in drinking it. During droughts or when bananas are scarce, Rwandans fall back on ikigage, a less tasty sorghum beer that is equally intoxicating.

† Ignace was seventy-one when he was released from prison. —Translator's note

our songs, so as not to spark attention. I thought deep down it was hard to believe that anyone could take pity on us, it just shouldn't be . . ."

The columns of prisoners follow a road cushioned in thick dust, through barren foothills colored yellow and gray instead of the ocher and green of the slopes of Nyamata. Watched by scrawny cows endlessly chewing their meager cuds in the shade of a few rare trees, the men advance, encountering women walking single file with jerry cans, going toward the only trickling stream for twenty kilometers around. Neither hunger nor thirst slows the steps of the former prisoners as they make their way in silence through this rocky landscape, dotted with shrubs and striped with fields of maize or sorghum at the edge of an occasional marsh or lake. Crossing a territory that was once home to elephants and lions driven out decades ago by waves of Tutsi refugees, who were themselves fleeing the wars in Burundi or the pogroms in the north, the men remember that this region of sand dunes later became the home base of the rebel troops of the Tutsi *inkotanyi* ("The Invincibles") before they went to war against the regime of President Habyarimana. These hardscrabble lands have been inhabited for several decades by families convinced that they have earned the privilege, in the arid desolation of their fields and the decrepitude of their rusting shacks, of escaping the ethnic fury of the surrounding areas.

In Nyamata, the chief town of the region, people are stupefied to learn of the prisoners' release. Among them are all those survivors of the genocide whom I had interviewed and reported on in my first book about Rwanda, *Life Laid Bare*. These veterans of the marshes of Nyamwiza and the forest of Kayumba well recall their shock at the news.

· · ·

Angélique Mukamanzi: "I heard the announcement on the radio. We had been growing used to our new future as survivors; household chores were sweeping bad thoughts into the hole of forgetfulness . . . We were rejoining life: time was coming around to our side. Suddenly, because of that bulletin, time switched camps. I felt my body shaking. Memories came crashing back pell-mell. We gathered throughout the *mudugudu* in little groups of friends, wondering how the killers would arrive.

"The first prisoners I saw were coming up the path to their homes as I was going down toward Nyamata. They avoided everyone's eyes. They tried to stay close together, in line, and crouched down to greet us on the path. Those men had cut so much with their machetes that they should well have died in their turn. That was my one and only thought."

Janvier Munyaneza: "Everyone marveled at their good health. They were clean, neat, and seemed to have put on weight. And later we noticed that work made them sweat in a strange way. You could tell it was fear making them behave nicely.

"The authorities had called us together to address us before the return of the prisoners—to prevent us from harassing or attacking them, to make us keep our accusations and hostility to ourselves until the *gaçaça* trials began. When Tutsi boys spoke loudly of revenge, the authorities snapped back that they might well find themselves replacing the prisoners in Rilima."

Claudine Kayitesi: "I went outside with the children to look at them; they were passing in single file with bundles on their heads. We exchanged no words. The children were scared, thinking that the prisoners would start plotting again. Personally, I was simply curious to see them. The first one I recognized was a neighbor named Cambarela—the very one who hacked up my big sister. As for them, their sheepish voices were saying, 'Hallelujah, hallelujah! How are you? May God protect you! Love one another as yourselves. We shall pray for you, that's definite from now on.' We stared at them, gaping, without lifting a finger."

The former prisoners have no time to unpack their bundles, because at home they find a summons waiting: they must leave immediately for a course in "civic reconciliation" in a reeducation camp in the Bicumbi region. This is how Alphonse describes that period: "They taught us how to conduct ourselves around the families who had suffered—to behave humbly, to appear timid in confrontations, to avoid provocation when facing distraught survivors. To avoid as well the disorders of AIDS and suchlike illnesses. To learn how to bake bricks for grieving widows or abandoned children.

"But the number-one lesson had to do with our wives. The instructors warned us that all the prisoners would run into epidemics of adultery, kids born on the sly, fields sold behind our backs. They taught us that since the government had pardoned us, we in turn had to pardon our unfaithful wives, who'd had no way of knowing we would ever leave prison alive, and who had taken up the hoe without a strong man to help shoulder their burdens.

"In prison, many detainees had been furious with their straying or spendthrift wives. They promised them the most dreadful fate, but the training personnel came down ferociously on this attitude. They drummed in the lesson: Remain calm with your guilty spouse, be peaceable with your neighbor, patient with those who are traumatized, obedient with the authorities. And don't delay in getting to work on clearing your overgrown fields."

. . .

At the end of the reeducation period, the prisoners set out for the hills of home once again, this time for good. Alphonse continues his account: "I left the camp with my bundle on my head and walked with whoever came along. In Nyamata, I became embroiled in questions on the main street and hurried to get away, to avoid attracting the evil eye. My wife welcomed me in the proper way. My children had grown, and wore smiles. We didn't celebrate with chicken, because of the neighbors: we didn't want to appear too pleased, so we cooked potatoes instead.

"Before, I owned several houses as well as a *cabaret*,* but my wife sold them. I'd had stocks of goods—all cleaned out by now, obviously. Right away I went to visit my property. Once it was a glorious field with flourishing banana plants; when I got there, I mourned a wasteland wilder than a pampa. I pruned a few surviving banana plants. I allowed myself two days of rest. Of course, I did have to wait nineteen days for the results of my AIDS test before taking my place as a husband.

"The center of town had lost its lively warmth and bustle. Poverty and discouragement had scoured all kind words from the little *cabarets*. Still, I could see that the two camps had been strictly disciplined. The Hutus had learned to curb their wickedness, the Tutsis to curb their resentment."

Pancrace: "Those without money for the truck walked off in a long line. Once in the bush, we sorted ourselves out by our

---

* *The Rwandan cabaret can be an authentic tavern, with a proper sign and terrace, but is often a humbler combination of social club, bar, and general store—perhaps a few thatched huts in someone's yard or a one-room shop with no sign, a floor of beaten earth, cases of beer and soft drinks stacked against a wall, bottles and cans of home-brewed banana and sorghum beer at the counter. It might stock a few groceries, some fabrics, household items, and hardware. A sofa or bench and some stools sit around a low table just inside the door for rainy weather, and patrons move their seats outside if it's sunny. Brochettes of goat meat smoke appetizingly on grills in the back courtyard, and patrons are welcome until late in the evening. —Translator's note*

hills. We held back on singing, but not on little yelps of high spirits.

"I had not set foot in Nyamata for nine years. I noticed the advertisement photos, the new makes of taxi-bus, the charred walls . . . The town seemed chaotic. We did not stop for drinks, so we could hurry on. The hugs with old friends began in Nyarunazi; I was eager to get home to put on nice-looking clothes. My sisters had bought *urwagwa* and special potato dishes—without meat, unfortunately. The family rejoiced. Still, I felt pangs of dismay at the dilapidation: holes in the metal roofing, the woodwork attacked by termites, the cracked cement. All the banana plants had perished.

"The next day I sat in the courtyard to receive visits from acquaintances. They wanted to know about our prison life, hear news of those who had not confessed, and learn above all which names had been mentioned at trial. Some people came to greet me in good faith, while others pretended to be pleasant, since they had truly hoped I would stay in prison. That night, the darkness closed in on me with worries; I waited until daybreak to visit my field. On the second day, swamp malaria caught up with me. I went straight back to farming anyway: I dug up stumps, ripped out brush. The routine had not changed, but my joints groaned with fatigue.

"At first, I hesitated to go up into town in Kibungo. I feared chance encounters, risky words. I waited a month, and then I downed my first Primus,* paid for by a neighbor. I'd been craving a beer; it was a most vexing longing in Rilima. I'd no longer dared imagine it, because time had held no hope of rescue.

"In the gang, friendship has not faltered: we meet up often,

---

* *Primus, a Belgian brand, is the most popular beer in Rwanda. Brewed in Gisenyi, near the Congo border, it is sold only in one-liter bottles, from which it is drunk lukewarm.*

except for Adalbert, who lives the bourgeois life in Kigali. Him, when he comes back here, he shows up in crisply creased suits. He offers drinks with a glad hand in the *cabaret*, and we chat freely.

"In prison we slept crowded on straw mattresses, with no room in our sleep for evil dreams. In prison we had forgotten the killings, I mean their upsetting feelings; we dreamed only of childhood memories, or of painful moments in prison, like the brawls or the sicknesses. Since our release, however, the killings have been cropping up in conversation, so dreams are coming back to gnaw at us. At home we sleep free, we sleep more truly, so the bad dreams reappear quite clearly: the house burnings, the hunting chases through the swamps, the blood in the marsh ponds, and above all, the people we ran after.

"I have not visited any survivors; I've been afraid of their traumas. We've met in passing, we've managed to greet one another without being nasty, and that's been enough for us. I have not noticed anything dangerous in people's eyes. Basically, I think we have been severely lectured on both sides.

"I was charged, I was convicted, I was pardoned. I did not ask to be forgiven. After all, it's not worth asking for forgiveness if your plea cannot be accepted."

Stunned, anxious when not plain terrified, the survivors await the repercussions of these returns. Months go by. Claudine describes her reactions: "Not one prisoner came asking for forgiveness. They are afraid to have a conversation, so if someone goes near them— quick, they blurt out a *bonjour* to ward off a handshake, behaving like angels but turning away from any gesture of closeness with us.

"I myself would have no trouble watching them be shot, one after the other, in public. They cut hard enough to break their own arms, in broad daylight. Forgiving them means nothing human. That may be the will of God, but not ours.

"When they got out, it was clear they had been chastised in prison; but changed . . . that's a different matter. Someone who grabbed the first chance to cut at that pace, he won't pass up another chance if a fresh war beckons him. Those first days, when they walked about freely, my dream came back: we were running, with killers at our heels; people were caught while I slipped away and, looking back, I saw those dead folks sitting down, chatting, and wanting nothing more to do with me. Later on I got used to the prisoners; my dream went away. You adjust to having them around."

Berthe Mwanankabandi: "Myself, I became so disturbed, so discouraged, that I left for Butare, where a prayer association found me day work as a ward girl in a hospital. I swore never to return here—I could not brave the hatred glaring in so many eyes. But as you see, I did come back.

"No one sent a message of apology or a little gift. They just don't care, or they fear recriminations. They think that since they were freed by order of the president of the republic, it's no longer in their interest to bend down or speak humbly to simple farmers. Basically, they believe they don't need to offer a proper apology anymore, because they didn't receive a proper punishment.

"The first prisoner I ran into was my best teacher, a man named Jean. And I was the one who was startled. He was wearing a fine suit. He did not say *bonjour*, and neither did I. I felt almost humiliated; I swerved to one side on the path."

Innocent Rwililiza:* "If you think about it, who is it talking about forgiveness? The Tutsis? The Hutus? The freed prisoners,

* *Innocent Rwililiza was a young teacher when his wife and little son were killed in the Nyamata church massacre. He became a trusted aide and interpreter for Jean Hatzfeld during the author's research in Nyamata. —Translator's note*

their families? None of them. It's the humanitarian organizations. They are importing forgiveness to Rwanda, and they wrap it in lots of dollars to win us over. There is a Forgiveness Plan just as there is an AIDS Plan, with public awareness meetings, posters, petty local presidents, super-polite Whites in all-terrain turbo vehicles. These humanitarian workers lecture our teachers, bring our communal councilors on board. They finance various assistance projects. As for us, we speak of forgiveness to earn their good opinion—and because the subsidies can be lucrative.

"But when we talk among ourselves, the word *forgiveness* has no place; I mean that it's oppressive. For example: You see Adalbert return. He led the killings on Kibungo Hill, he was pardoned, he parades around Kigali, he wields his machete once more in his fields. You, you're from Kibungo, living five hundred meters from his house, and you lost your mama, papa, two sisters, wife, and little boy. You run into Adalbert downtown. He to you, you to him—who's going to say that word *forgiveness*? It's outside of nature. The times we live in just shove everything down our throats."

Jeannette Ayinkamiye: "Letting them out of the penitentiary, that could be accepted because the fields cried out for workers, but first they should have paid compensation to the victims. We simply could not understand freeing them so one-sidedly. We wondered, What's going on again? The authorities help out the Hutus without a thought for us: they don't even see us anymore. Since we could not show our anger, we made jokes. When you get right down to it, we said, luck loves the Hutus: they kill and are not killed; they flee to Congo and are brought home for free; they go to prison and come out fat and rested; they burn our homes and find their own waiting nicely for them with their wives inside to tend the cooking fire and open their arms at night."

Ignace, the oldest of the band of killers: "In the first days of freedom, farmwork is tiring. It's the palms of the hands that suffer. The chest cannot keep up the pace anymore. After two months the arms recover the habits of a lifetime. I began with repairs on the house: the framework, the broken tiles. I planted sweet potatoes and beans. I get up at five, I go straight to my fields; at noon I eat some beans and nap on my bench. I return to the fields, I come home at about five o'clock. I wash and go stroll around until nightfall. We haven't gotten back to the level of farming from before the killings, but we're trying to revive the basic crops.

"My wife, Spéciose, died while I was in prison. My daughter tried to take over the family land during my incarceration, and I was forced to clear her off. I had to remarry: I was struggling to manage all by myself. The sowing, the hoe work, household chores . . . I was having trouble eating and sleeping alone. Solitude stores up only bad thoughts. It's easier to live in prison, among friends, than alone on a plot of land with just your painful memories. I enlisted a paternal uncle as go-between; he found a mama with two children. She came by, she visited my plot of land. She seems content, since she's not mentioning any problems.

"That first day, I got my hands on a bottle of *urwagwa*: The drink was tasty, yet my belly felt too weak to finish it. Besides, we'd been forbidden to get drunk.

"Our young men behaved more boldly on our expeditions, so they have problems with the Tutsis. As for me, no worry: I feel comfortable, I received a cow as a welcome gift, even though I'm Hutu, and I have not been bothered or reproached."

. . .

Sylvie Umubyeyi*: "I thought, Thousands of Tutsi widows have arms too weak to raise a hoe; from now on they sweat out both man's and woman's work in the fields, getting no help to feed their children, and here are thousands of Hutu women given the gift of a man's two strong arms. The wickedest women are receiving the best reward. When I telephoned Butare, in my native region, I heard, 'Here, too, a catastrophe is brewing. Everyone's talking about it. The survivors raise their voices in anger. The authorities are threatening those who speak out of line. Fragile survivors are collapsing in anguish. Your cousin, she's making herself sick over it.'

"One day I heard a commotion outside. I slipped into a small crowd on the main street. When we saw the first prisoners appear in the distance, it was '94 all over again. We stood there, trembling. They came closer. They passed by in a line, acting timid or ashamed, keeping quiet, very well trained. They went on without ever looking back, they disappeared, and we, we were no longer afraid.

"That afternoon a gentleman came into the bakery holding a little boy by the hand. He ordered a Fanta soda and a sweet snack roll for him. He was sweating. He had just gotten out of prison and moved like an old man. When we chatted, he said, 'I'm sad now because I have a son I haven't watched grow up. Because I was a strong man and have become a weakling. I was a respectable person and no one greets me anymore. Evil has ruined my life.'

"I thought, Fine, this man is speaking sincerely. If all the

---

* Fleeing from the university town of Butare, where many of their relatives were slaughtered when the genocide began, Sylvie Umubyeyi, her husband, and their two children eventually wound up in Nyamata. There, Sylvie became a social worker; she was the first person to help Jean Hatzfeld in his quest to interview survivors of the genocide. —Translator's note

Hutus went wrong, each and every Hutu, what could be the point of learning what this one did in particular? If he shows remorse or offers to be friends with me, I'll say yes from my heart, because life must go on. He kept speaking plaintively about his misfortunes, saying courteous things in a pitiful voice, but he neither asked for nor offered anything. These people cannot take us into consideration, cannot ask for our forgiveness. Why? I don't know."

A FATAL REVELATION

Seven years earlier, on a morning when a yellowish mist still lingered over the sea of tents and shacks in a refugee camp at the foot of the Karisimbi volcano in eastern Congo, a revelation stopped Léopord Twagirayezu dead in his tracks.

Dropping the sack of flour he'd been carrying on his shoulder, flailing his arms to push everyone in the alley out of his way, Léopord dashed frantically to the church, a mud hut shored up by tree trunks, roofed with foliage, and identifiable as a holy place thanks only to the religious images cut from a parish calendar and glued to the outside walls. He rushed to the altar to pray, sang his head off with the worshippers gathered there, and knelt in the light of the morning sun. But it was no use. He could not drive away his vision, neither then nor later that evening nor in the days that followed. So he began to talk out loud. He spouted harangues filled with marshes, machetes, great spurts of blood. He started accusing himself in public of crimes, then began predicting punishment for whomever he happened to meet.

Léopord's reputation as a dangerous *interahamwe* had followed him to Congo. Gun in hand, a cartridge belt slung across his chest, he trained guerrilla commandos on the slopes of the volcano; he also circulated in the camp alleys, supervising the humanitarian organizations' distributions of oil and salt. His sudden diatribes were therefore quite surprising, but since they provoked no altercations, people became used to them, especially since everyone already knew about the murders to which he was confessing; and anyway, crackpot preachers were cropping up all through the camp.

Around 25,000 Hutus had been living for sixteen months on that plain in the Masisi area, ever since their exodus from Rwanda after the end of the genocide in 1994: columns of women carrying children or bundles of household goods, kids driving livestock, old folks leaning on staves, all in a forced march across the countryside, escorted by journalists and photographers, sometimes helped along their way, making for the Sebeya River, which they crossed under the watchful eye of elite French troops, reaching Goma at last under the protection of humanitarian organizations. From there they finally fanned out across the plains and plateaus of Kivu.

Léopord came from Muyange Hill, a dozen kilometers from Nyamata; he and his family had left there in a horrific panic early on the afternoon of May 14. Already armed with his cartridge belt and machete, he, like other *interahamwe*, escorted the Hutu clans during their flight into exile.

Léopord and his four sisters were born in Muyange, where his father owned a large tract of land. A docile but poor student in school, he was a whirlwind of energy outside the classroom. According to his mother, Xavérine Nyirabuseruka, "He was a strapping boy, quite robust, who never got sick, seemed big for his age, and was tireless out in the fields."

As an adolescent he grew tall and well muscled without becoming stocky. All in a day's work, he attended to the family plot through the afternoon, then hired himself out in the surrounding fields and sometimes went woodcutting in the forest for pocket money he spent gaily in the *cabaret*. A tenor in the church choir, he left off working and drinking on Sundays, when he never skipped Mass in his black suit and tie. He picked out for himself one of the prettiest girls in the neighborhood and, after a festive wedding, took her home to his field. "He lived along the fourth road of our farming community, and I was on the fifth," a neighbor, Mélanie Mukakabera, remembers. "I saw him every day; he went around like a wandering Hercules. Nothing— difficulties, brushwood, neighbors—dared stand up to him. He was shy, not a bad guy, but his temper would blaze up in a flash."

In April 1994, along with almost all other Hutus like him, he joined the party of President Juvénal Habyarimana as a matter of course. Learning of the attack on the president's plane, however, he was among the very first Hutus to gather in excited groups on his hill, and "straightaway he found his place at the center to shout for vengeance," says his neighbor Mélanie. Naturally, when the massacres began, he was at the head of a gang in the market at Nyamata. Later, in the Rilima penitentiary, he spoke of the day it all started.

"That day was clearly destined to heat up. I took my machete and went to the center of town. On every side I saw people giving chase. At the marketplace a man came running toward me. He was racing down from Kayumba, all breathless and scared, looking only for escape: In passing, I gave him a machete blow at neck level, on the vulnerable vein. It came to me naturally, without thinking. He made no defensive move—he fell without shouting, without moaning. I felt nothing, just let him lie. I looked around; killing was going on every which way. I kept pursuing the other fugitives all day long . . . It was sweaty-hard and stimulating, like an unexpected diversion. I didn't bother to keep count . . . At the time of those murders I considered them unimportant and didn't even notice the tiny thing that would change me into a killer."

Shortly afterward Léopord added, "We no longer considered the Tutsis as humans or even as creatures of God. We had stopped seeing the world as it is, I mean as an expression of God's will. So we found it easy to wipe them out. That's why those of us who prayed in secret did so for ourselves, never for our victims."

Let's return to the Congolese camp, three months after Léopord's vision. He continued to harangue the crowd and proclaim his guilt until one November night in 1996, when the forces of the Rwandan Patriotic Front surged out of the darkness, surrounded the camp in Kivu, and launched an artillery attack. As abruptly as they had fled their native hills, the Hutu refugees, panicked by the shelling, stampeded into the only corridor left open by the soldiers of Paul Kagame: a path leading directly back to Rwanda. An immense procession of people pouring from all the camps on the plateaus formed up and, harassed by the troops from Kigali, headed for home.

Léopord had hardly returned to Muyange when he was locked up in the communal jail along with other bit players. He expected to be executed, because during his two years in exile, stories told by the survivors of the marshes had given him a bloodthirsty reputation.

During his first interrogation by the public prosecutor's office, however, Léopord sprang a surprise. Unlike his peers, who lied for all they were worth, defending themselves by denying everything, Léopord—haunted by his revelation—told all. Even more forthcoming than in the camp, where he had preached remorse to an amused audience, he told the prosecutors about the killing expeditions, listed names, described the planning, the various episodes, never ducked a question, didn't try to exonerate himself.

Why him? Why, in that community of deceit, amnesia, and

silence, did he open the floodgates of his memory? Why did he, unlike his pals, simply stop scheming? In a critical review of Jonathan Littell's novel *Les Bienveillantes* (*The Kindly Ones*), Claude Lanzmann, director of *Shoah*, the celebrated documentary film about the Holocaust, emphasizes the contrast between the novel's hero, Max Aue (an SS officer who "talks nonstop for nine hundred pages, this man who no longer knows what a memory is [yet] remembers absolutely everything . . . he talks like a book, like all the history books Littell has read"), and the actual SS soldiers whom Lanzmann himself could not persuade to speak in a normal way when he was making his film. And in his fascinating book *Ordinary Men*, the historian Christopher Browning describes even more precisely how policemen in a battalion of reservists from Hamburg, who were responsible during the Second World War for the killing and deportation of tens of thousands of Polish and Russian Jews, proved incapable of speaking about their crimes. What does Léopord's talkativeness mean, then? Does it challenge Browning's argument about the more or less fundamental "negationism" of the Nazi criminals? Not necessarily, since the context of Léopord's confessions and the very nature of his expiatory accounts preclude comparison to the situation of the police reservists, as we shall see. Still, Léopord did talk, and he went over his story whenever he was asked to and even when he wasn't, because no one could stop him.

At Rilima, he said, "Some try to show remorse but tremble before the truth . . . As for me, it was in a camp in Congo that I first felt my heart ache. I prayed, hoping to find relief, but in vain. After every prayer or hymn, shame would lie in wait for me. So I began being sorry out loud, ignoring the mockery of my comrades. In prison I told my whole truth. It came out freely. Ever since then, whenever someone asks me for it, it flows the same way."

He repeated his confessions at his trial; he gave evidence before several tribunals; he told his story to foreign visitors drawn by his notoriety. His cooperation with the authorities spared him a death sentence, and even better, the sentence was commuted to seven years in prison, a shorter term than his cell mates received. Which didn't stem the tide: his confessions became an inexhaustible logorrhea of repentance, and began to have repercussions.

One day, for example, he left prison to speak at a public information meeting about the revival of the *gaçaça* courts, in a village near his home. The mikes were set up on the podium; a crowd awaited him. Clad in his pink prisoner's uniform, swinging his shoulders like a knight in shining armor, he stepped up to speak, confident of success. To his astonishment, his words set off an immediate barrage of shouts and insults from Tutsis outraged by his crimes and Hutus incensed by what they saw as his self-serving denunciations. Léopord was taken back to prison, stunned, yet even more determined than ever.

Shortly afterward he explained: "It is awkward to speak of forgiveness in prison. Outside, if I receive a tornado of fury instead of forgiveness, I will not show any spite . . . I will simply tell people, All right: forgiveness, now it belongs to you, it's on your side, you have certainly earned it. So from now on you can handle it however you like. Me, I can wait for your right moment. I will pick up my life again where it left off without muttering against you."

Neither the shock of that first stormy confrontation with the people on his hill nor the threats of his fellow detainees, whose trial was approaching, convinced Léopord to keep quiet. On the contrary, with the help of a pal who had better writing skills, he consigned his accounts of the killings to a school notebook. He drew columns, listing the names of his victims and the dates and zones of the major expeditions, and he strongly underlined the action of his confederates along with tallies of their victims.

Released from the penitentiary along with Pio, Pancrace, Alphonse, and the other members of their band, Léopord ventured to return discreetly to his hill. His wife had left him for a less problematic farmer. On his own, he cleared the invasive brush from his land, and since that wasn't enough for him, he went off to do woodcutting or charcoal burning in the eucalyptus forests. At night, he quenched his thirst in a *cabaret*.

"He had no sense of his own strength," says Évariste Niyibizi, the municipal councilor in Muyange, a man who knew Léopord from way back. "He did everything at full tilt. If you asked him to work or sing, he was there in the front line; if you asked him to kill, he was again in the front line, and same thing for the confessions: denounce, drink, char wood—he was always the most conscientious and enthusiastic in action."

Léopord set up house with a neighbor, Bazizane Nyiradende, a Twa woman whose family were charcoal burners in the forest.* She was an habituée of the *urwagwa* dives of Nyamata, and the couple's epic benders became the stuff of legend in the neighborhood, for the lovers squabbled at night as fiercely as they worked by day and tippled in the evening.

When the committees of preliminary investigation for the *gaçaça* courts began to deal with the commune of Nyamata,† they

---

* *The diminutive Twa—called Bakas in Gabon, Mbutis in Congo, Akkas in the Central African Republic—are also commonly known as Pygmies. The third and by far the smallest ethnic group in Rwanda, they make up only a fraction of 1 percent of the population. Neglected by Tutsi and Hutu regimes alike, they shun the cities for Rwanda's dense rain forests, where they keep to themselves, working at traditional crafts. During the genocide, the* interahamwe *exterminated almost a third of them.*

† *At the communal or town level the* gaçaça *courts arraign the accused in the community where the crime took place and local citizens give testimony or pass judgment under the supervision of court officers.*

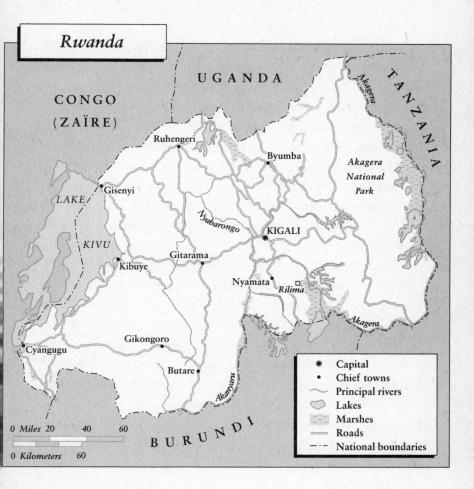

Rwanda

UGANDA

CONGO
(ZAÏRE)

TANZANIA

Ruhengeri

Byumba

Akagera

Gisenyi

Akagera
National
Park

LAKE

Nyabarongo

KIGALI

KIVU

Gitarama

Kibuye

Nyamata   Rilima

Akagera

Gikongoro

Cyangugu

Butare

Akanyaru

BURUNDI

⊙	Capital
●	Chief towns
∿	Principal rivers
	Lakes
	Marshes
	Roads
–·–	National boundaries

0 Miles 20   40   60

0 Kilometers   60

were confronted by the lies of the killers and their relatives and by the imprecise testimony of survivors who—in hiding or running for their lives—had not always witnessed murders with their own eyes. These committees turned to the inexhaustible accounts offered by Léopord, who was eager to continue his role as pitiless accuser, not only before the judges but also in the marketplace and *cabarets*. He even publicly threatened his mother with his accusations. "People said that Léopord didn't hesitate to barter his testimony from *cabaret* to *cabaret*," asserts Marie-Louise Kagoyire. "When he was drunk and became angry, he'd threaten to denounce a guy, to make him buy him a Mutzig, the most expensive beer," confirms Mélanie Mukakabera. "And yet," she adds, "God knows he was never caught out boasting or bearing false witness."

And that's what worried or panicked a good number of his former machete-wielding accomplices. Three of them in particular tried repeatedly to placate him and then moved on to threats. Their names appear in the complaints Léopord filed with Évariste, the municipal councilor: "He came often because he sensed the danger. He said he would definitely be murdered soon, because many of his old colleagues were grumbling about him. Three especially complained more than the rest: a certain Sebutura offered him some fine goats before confronting him; a man named Misigaro proposed a nice sum of money; one Nzaramba was quite insistent. That last was the worst, because he's powerful: he teaches at the university in Kigali and was afraid of losing his position."

On the evening of September 15, 2004, Léopord returned from the market. A neighbor called to him from the *mudugudu*, holding out a bottle of Primus; his wife, Bazizane, shouted at him to come home and eat; a raucous, drunken spat broke out in the couple's courtyard. Then Bazizane ran cursing to her brother's house, pursued by Léopord. Two shots rang out in the darkness. Léopord fell with one bullet through his temple and another through his heart. A professional job.

Hearing the news, his mama immediately rushed into the courtyard to accuse her daughter-in-law, "and above all to try getting her hands on the school notebook, which I had already confiscated," says Councilor Évariste, who had arrived at the scene two minutes earlier.

Because the couple had often quarreled and had been fighting only a few minutes before the murder, and doubtless because she was a Twa and an alcoholic, Bazizane spent six months in jail before being released. The investigators later admitted that it was impossible to imagine her turning a gun on her companion while in full drunken flight. The two farmers and the university professor mentioned in Léopord's complaints were called in. The first two were locked up but set free for lack of proof; the third man had a cast-iron alibi.

If not they, who? Gunned down by one of his innumerable Tutsi victims' relatives, infuriated by his notoriety and bravado as a great killer/drinker/informer? Disposed of by a Hutu threatened by his accusations? Assassinated by order of a former policeman or soldier, by a leading citizen or rich merchant? For lack of proof, Councilor Évariste has filed the dossier away with other unsolved cases. "In any case," he remarks, "it was in fact the Tutsis who were saddened by the murder, because they are always on the lookout for more secrets and had hoped to hear many new revelations at the *gaçaça* trials from Léopord's lips. In many *cabarets* it was the Hutus who sang and caroused in remarkable bacchanals, celebrating with brochettes of roast meat and whole cases of Primus."

What do his pals think, the men with whom he hunted Tutsis in the marshes, then shared prison quarters in Rilima? Pancrace Hakizamungili, for example, who arrived this morning at the market on his bike to sell a sack of manioc, smiles at the question before answering.

"Léopord, he proved himself outstanding in killing. He wanted to be outstanding in gossip and denunciations. Everything he said was true, recounted in full, with all the details lined up the right way. But who can bear that? The things he said were so truthful, they could turn diabolical. And in the new atmosphere of national reconciliation, they became too much."

IN KAYUMBA

Leaving Kigali these days, one no longer sees the cloud of dust that streams of trucks and taxi-buses once raised above the doughnut stands, *igisoro** players, throngs of travelers, and gas station shanties. This cloud over the capital's main avenue once marked the turnoff to a rutted dirt road heading south toward the Bugesera, but a German company has leveled and paved that road, which now runs smoothly across the region, connects with the main street of Nyamata, and continues straight on to the Burundi border. No more potholes, flats, crapped-out suspension systems, bruised buttocks, parched throats. Farewell to travelers overburdened with bundles, waiting to clamber onto the back of an exhausted vehicle laboring up a hill or forced to a halt by a herd of dawdling cows.

Two hours' drive down the road, at the edge of the Nyabarongo River, a concrete span has now replaced the former metal footbridge, which used to periodically shed wobbly plates into the water, allowing time for women farming in nearby fields to run over to sell *urwagwa* to dusty travelers or peddle their crops

---

* Isigoro *(familiar to American children as* mancala*) belongs to the worldwide family of "sowing games"—and is as hard to win as it is easy to play. Two players compete, ideally at lightning speed, in collecting and distributing little stones or seeds along a series of holes arranged in two or four rows on a board, until one player has captured all the pieces.*

to the merchants stuck in line waiting for the bridge to be repaired. The new bridge is a less haphazard landmark for the entrance to the district of Nyamata.

But the marshy waters remain as colorful as ever, thanks to giant water lilies and colonies of ibises and egrets. At dawn, before the road traffic picks up, you can see herds of stocky black hippopotami returning swiftly on stubby legs to their muddy homes after a night of browsing on grasses. Beyond these wild riverbanks lie extensive plantations of dark green sugarcane recently bought up by investors such as the former Rwandan ambassador to France and local businessmen like Chicago, the biggest beer wholesaler in Nyamata.

Farther on—as far as the eye can see—stretch swamps from which rise swirls of mist, flights of birds, and the raucous whistling of long-tailed *talapoins*, acrobatic little monkeys quite at home in this watery world. These marshes surround the fourteen hills of Nyamata: to the north and east, the bogs of Butamwa along the Nyabarongo River; on the west, those of Nyamwiza along the Akanyaru; and to the south, the swamps of Murago on the shores of Lake Cyohoha. It was in these marshes that tens of thousands of Tutsis sought refuge when the massacres began on April 11, 1994. An equal number hid in hilltop forests, particularly in Kayumba.

In *Life Laid Bare* and *Machete Season* I told the story of the killings in the marshes, those vast stretches of slime and papyrus inhabited by snakes, wild pigs, and *sitatungas*.* I described the ordeal of Tutsis who spent their days crouching or lying in muck beneath the swamp foliage and their nights grubbing for food in

---

* *This extraordinary antelope of amphibious habits has an oily, water-repellent coat and slender, splayed-out hoofs that allow it to run swiftly through mire but make its gait on dry land somewhat ungainly. The* sitatunga *feeds at dawn and dusk on papyrus leaves, and in case of danger can hide for hours submerged in water with only its nose showing.*

abandoned fields, and the hunting expeditions of Hutus who assembled each morning on a soccer field, then set out singing to wade knee-deep through mire, lifting up branches with one hand and hacking their victims into pieces with the other, just the way they had always pruned their banana plants. If I barely mentioned the killings in Kayumba Forest, this was not because they were less appalling or less worthy of historical record. The reason was simple: in the swamps, thousands of Tutsis survived the massacres, in which thousands of their Hutu neighbors took part. All those people today share memories of that hell—memories with which they must live together from now on.

But almost no Tutsis emerged alive from the forests, where many Hutus came from far away to hunt them. So bearing witness is an altogether different proposition here. The forest episode of the genocide seemed like a story within a story, something separate, and I stashed it away in a corner of my memory until the day when two chance encounters during a recent trip to Nyamata inspired me to reconsider it. Médiatrice and Eugénie were among the very rare survivors of the manhunts in Kayumba, and the only women among those few. Médiatrice is a girl I met in Marie-Louise Kagoyire's living room when she dropped in to say hello on the last day of school; I met Eugénie, a young woman, one afternoon on the terrace of Marie-Louise's *cabaret* in Kanzenze, The Widows' Corner, where it's always good to stop by when coming down from Kibungo.

In a recent novel, one character—a war correspondent and sometime writer who feels uneasy returning to Paris after a long stint in battle zones—has this to say: "Literature isn't something that comes naturally, it's a thing born of haphazard opportunities and coincidence . . . of confrontations, serendipitous jumbles . . . It's a crowd of characters and events that the author puts together as chance encounters dictate and that no historian will ever reconstruct. Literature may be a kind of willful wandering within what happened, the traces this leaves . . . Writing down this transformation is literature."

Such traces and encounters have given rise to this third book composed in Nyamata, where the reader will find once more, a few years later, everyone from the first two accounts, along with the ghosts who now keep them company and meddle in their startling confrontations.

FOREST EXPLOITS

From a row of seriously decrepit bars behind the main square in Nyamata, alleys climb steeply up through the neighborhood of Kayumba on the hill of that name, which overhangs the clustered dwellings. Many school principals, judges, and bureaucrats have built their homes here to enjoy the soft breezes offering relief from the suffocating heat below.

Halfway up the slope, beyond the last houses, the alleys become forest paths that lead to the top of the hill. It's in this forest, during the killing season, that Eugénie Kayierere gave the most prodigious athletic performance of which this former sports reporter has ever heard—a heroic accomplishment more difficult to imagine than any feat of navigation or mountain climbing. Indeed, it's simply a triumph beyond human understanding.

Eugénie is not the only person to have shown such prowess, since twenty people out of six thousand survived the hunting expeditions in Kayumba Forest. Aside from Médiatrice, however—then a desperate little eleven-year-old who sneaked back down the hill after twelve days to lose herself amid the Hutu population of Nyamata—the other survivors were sturdy fellows of about thirty, men in their prime and conditioned by farmwork or even athletics.

Eugénie, though, hadn't run since she was a tot, until she

began those five weeks of mad dashes, sprints, leaps, and marathon races that amaze her even today: "You found yourself doing unbelievable things you just couldn't begin to explain to anyone. Not even to yourself . . . like tripping over a stump, rolling through three somersaults, then blasting off in a zigzaggy sprint to escape for one last instant from the hiss of the machetes swiping at your back."

The Kayumba Forest is a sparse one, with growths of thorny shrubs and stunted eucalyptus trees whose roots crawl and tangle up with one another in their struggle to penetrate the flinty red dirt. On any ordinary day, the cowherds and the animals they drive up there—not so much to let them graze, since the brushwood is mostly indigestible, as to give them some shade—are the only creatures around, except for the eagles soaring far overhead in infinite circles.

At the summit, the view to the south encompasses the sheet-metal roofs of Nyamata gleaming in the sunshine (tiny and scattered among patches of farmland, larger and closer together in town) and, in the distance, the burnt-yellow plain of Maranyundo, bordered by mountainous ridges. To the northwest one can see fields, then the first stretches of marshland, backed up by the hills of Ntarama, Kibungo, and Kanzenze. It was from that direction that Eugénie fled to Kayumba, whereas Innocent raced up to the forest from Nyamata.

Both their accounts, which are vital to the message of this book, begin on the first day of the killings. Eugénie left her house in Kanzenze to hide in the forest, which was fifteen kilometers away: "When we saw the first homes go up in flames, my husband and I ran for our lives; we lost track of each other in the panic. I followed some neighbors. We wound up surrounded by *interahamwe* in the bush, where we lay low for four days, without moving even to relieve ourselves, before setting out again. I was

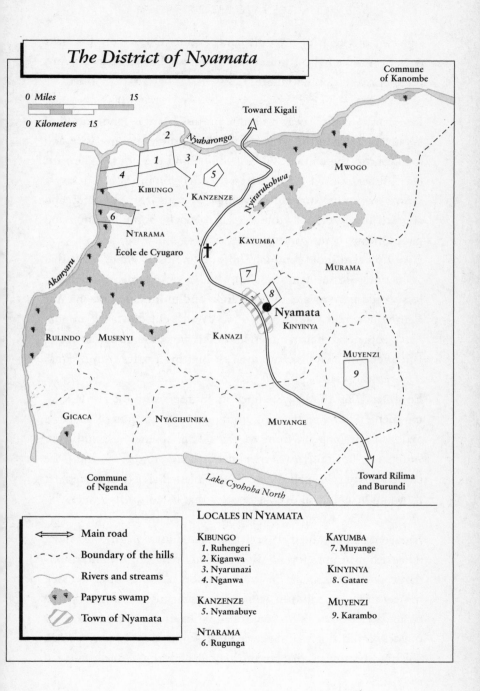

The District of Nyamata

0 Miles 15

0 Kilometers 15

Commune of Kanombe

Toward Kigali

Nyabarongo

2

1

3

5

4

KIBUNGO

KANZENZE

6

NTARAMA

École de Cyugaro

Nyirarukobwa

MWOGO

KAYUMBA

MURAMA

7

8

Nyamata

KINYINYA

Akanyaru

RULINDO

MUSENYI

KANAZI

MUYENZI

9

GICACA

NYAGIHUNIKA

MUYANGE

Commune of Ngenda

Lake Cyohoha North

Toward Rilima and Burundi

Main road

Boundary of the hills

Rivers and streams

Papyrus swamp

Town of Nyamata

LOCALES IN NYAMATA

KIBUNGO
1. Ruhengeri
2. Kiganwa
3. Nyarunazi
4. Nganwa

KANZENZE
5. Nyamabuye

NTARAMA
6. Rugunga

KAYUMBA
7. Muyange

KINYINYA
8. Gatare

MUYENZI
9. Karambo

right on the heels of my girlfriend Vestine. Quite early the next day, we reached the summit of the forest. Six thousand, a vast number, were camping there."

Innocent Rwililiza, near his home in the Gatare neighborhood of Nyamata: "When the mayor refused to protect us, my wife and son went to the church, while I hid behind the house. The next day, soldiers closed off all access to the church. When I saw a crowd going up toward Kayumba Forest, I went along and reached the woods at around eight o'clock. Some six thousand people were there, waiting.

"We heard shouts and gunshots in Nyamata. We thought that as in other ethnic flare-ups, only the people targeted on death lists would have to die, the rich folks and prominent citizens. We figured it would take two or three days to cut down the important people and their families, and then we could go home again. But after three days we saw the first hunting parties coming up."

Eugénie: "The youths were lined up in front, with the rest following them. They were coming from behind us, meaning Kanzenze, and also climbing up from Murama Hill, to the east, and from Nyamata. Obviously we were being attacked on all sides. We began running through the forest. That lasted all day, and the next morning it started all over again, and that lasted for five weeks."

Innocent: "They used to arrive at about nine in the morning. They'd hunt until eleven. We'd take advantage of the little midday rest. They'd return in the afternoon. Around three o'clock some minor expeditions would join them just to polish off the wounded. Those of us who hadn't been cut down by four o'clock could hope to make it through the day. At five o'clock we'd be sure of it. That meant life, all night long. We could tell the daily manhunt was over from the bickering and joking of the killers, the loot they carried off on their heads, and the bleating of the goats they drove before them. Sometimes expeditions returning from the marshes would pass by Kayumba on their way home, to put in a little extra effort. For us, too, that would mean a little extra: more running, more corpses. We ran for about six hours during the day. Some days threatened more than others, but never, never, was there a day without an attack."

Eugénie: "We'd drink in the evening. It was the rainy season in the beginning; the roofs still had their sheet metal,* which was more practical, because just tipping it made water trickle off. After the looters stripped the roofs, we licked tree leaves, and the brave went down to the backwaters of the Nyabarongo. We began foraging: manioc in the abandoned fields, and sweet potatoes. The strongest brought back provisions for the weakest. Evenings, we began by taking inventory of those we'd seen killed, how they'd been mutilated, and how we'd escaped the attacks. Basically, we spoke only of death, of the killers, and of the departed of the day. We'd speak softly until sleep caught us.

"Before daylight, we came out of the underbrush. Those who could went off to relieve themselves and then we'd go up to the top of the forest to rejoin the other refugees. Young lookouts would climb into the trees. The Hutus used to form two very long lines, between a thousand and two thousand killers. They'd come up calmly, no talking. Once they'd reached the flank of the

* In Machete Season, Hatzfeld devotes an entire chapter to corrugated metal, which the Belgians brought to Rwanda after the First World War to use as roofing for their buildings; with time, it became the roofing of choice for even the most modest dwelling, the terre-tôle, or "sheet metal/adobe" house. Used as a unit of measure (a house of "ten sheets") and exchange (a nanny goat costs two sheets), sheet metal is the only element of a house that villagers cannot make themselves, for rainy Rwanda does not provide thatching material. In 1994, sheet metal pillaged from Tutsi houses and then abandoned by exhausted Hutus fleeing into Congo was sometimes collected by Tutsi survivors struggling to rebuild their homes. — Translator's note

mountain, they began singing to terrorize us, and they certainly did. The most frightened among us would take off first and be the first to be tracked. Everywhere, people were running. We ran in small groups, depending on acquaintance, on courage, on whomever you'd spent the night with . . . The hunters, they dogged our heels, picking off the ones they could catch.

"In the beginning, it was fun for the killers, because they had no trouble cutting in great numbers. The first victims were the mamas and their babies, and the old folks, then the women and their desperate little children . . . The mamas and their nursing infants didn't last more than two or three days.

"We started out with six thousand and finished with twenty.

"Obviously, not all were cut on Kayumba; some were trapped while trying to reach the river or when making their way toward Burundi.

"We made friends in the evening shelters. We slept in small groups; there were some intimacies, even so. And in the morning, friends would run together. We knew one another very well. If you ran alone, you were caught quick; you became too vulnerable as prey. But in groups, we shared advice, we confused our pursuers. Some in the groups knew the bush: there'd be one who'd shout encouragements, another who'd spot the tricks and traps, one who'd be the strongest out front all day, and someone else the next day. You had to latch onto a gang that kept up its morale. Boys who had been herders or bandits—they became leaders who were very, very valuable.

"And when the killers seemed to be upon us, we'd scatter in all directions to give everyone a chance: basically, we adopted the antelope's strategy."

Innocent: "Me, I was in a group of six. I fell in with them by chance the first day. I was climbing up to Kayumba on my own when I was attacked by some killers; I ran, I happened upon this group at the end of my race, and they welcomed me. They were in their early thirties. Among them were a herdsman, a nice guy, quite familiar with the area; a truck driver, a truly courageous boy; a robust farmer; a boy who'd been a soldier in Uganda. We always ran together, in the same direction, keeping an eye on one another, scattering, calling to one another, regrouping.

"I stuck with them because they ran so swiftly and were experts on the slopes, trails, hiding places: 'Here behind these abandoned houses, the forest is thick; over there's a ditch . . .' The ex-soldier knew war strategies: hiding stock-still; not blundering into a trap; avoiding open country; detecting ambushes. Thanks to him, we started out with six and we finished with six, among the final twenty.

"Today those six have broken up, and the friendship along with it. We don't get together; we've never gone up to Kayumba Forest to walk side by side among the trees, search out the paths we ran on and recall certain moments, or just look around in silence. Not once. We've never shared brochettes in a *cabaret* to talk over memories good and bad. We prefer to find friends among people who weren't in our special gang, other survivors from the marshes or anywhere else. Why? I don't know.

"We six manage just in time to steer clear of one another. If I notice the herdsman passing in his car, he blows his horn, we call out friendly greetings, and he goes on his way. Each of us has taken responsibility for his own life. We're a little ashamed of that; I can't explain it. We're using a touch of camouflage . . . I think we want to show one another that we've gotten over everything."

Eugénie: "You had to dash away faster than the killers. One hunting party was pursuing you, another was lying in ambush a few kilometers away: you had to dogleg, double back, swerve around, without ever slowing down.

"Speed was fundamental, but so was morale. From the get-go, if your morning start lacked punch, you'd lost the match: your sprinting, dodging, leaping, wouldn't be the same. You had to team up with young people who would cheer up your heart. People whose hopes flagged—you could tell they would die that day or the next. Anyway, the most important thing wasn't your legs or wind or even your morale: it was really luck. You could be the fastest and shrewdest, with fantastic spirit, and fall beneath the machete blades in the first attack of the day. Many boys tougher than I was were cut through sheer bad luck.

"One time I stumbled on a bunch of killers eating chicken their wives were cooking for them over a fire, to build up their strength. The women had come along behind their men to gather sorghum and catch stray poultry. The killers grabbed their machetes. An old mama cursed me out just as a hunter was raising his blade to cut my neck. Behind him, a mama burst out crying at the top of her lungs, and the man's face turned toward her, scolding her. I seized my chance and escaped. I was saved by someone weeping. Weeping about what? I have no idea. Another day I was trapped by a neighbor I'd known for a long time. Our eyes locked so suddenly that his first blow missed me, and I ran off.

"Me, I ran barefoot, stabbing my feet on prickly brush. Wicked thorns made my legs swell. I was afraid they might go numb and refuse to move, so sometimes I had to stay crouched in a thicket for a day or two, absolutely still, waiting to get better, with no chance of a drop of water. Hoping not to be found out."

Innocent: "One day I was catching my breath beside a mama; we were leaning back against a rock. When the killers pounced on us from behind, I took off. One boy chased me faster than the others; he was really something. I could hear him panting—but out of nowhere I tripped, tumbling down a slope of thick bushes. Losing track of me under the branches, the boy cursed and grumbled and finally went hunting elsewhere. Another time I ran into some killers coming out of a field of maize. It was so abrupt, so close: I was truly done for. Okay: I put two five-hundred franc bills I'd brought from home down on the ground, and I sped away. The killers didn't chase me. They could have easily taken the money and me as well. You can evaluate morale, speed, or the people you knew in the forest, but luck, well, that's incalculable."

Eugénie: "I was wearing a *pagne* and a T-shirt. Every morning I had to roll the *pagne* up to my waist and secure it; that freed my legs, supported my back, and helped dull my hunger pangs. I wasn't ashamed at all. We knew perfectly well it didn't matter who saw us, and that gossip now went begging for ears. We felt already among the dead. We were no longer completely human anymore; I mean, we knew that we would certainly all die and that no one would reproach or jeer at us . . . Besides, whenever we could take a little break, men and women used to strip and start delousing one another. We were being eaten alive by lice, tormented by scabs, living like animals, and there was no time to feel ashamed.

"Before, I'd been lazy about running, I was a farmer. The fields never once even gave me cause to run. For a Rwandan woman, running is most improper and can make men angry, but when I ran with young men in the forest they never outpaced me. It was a true hunt: we darted helter-skelter through the woods, leaping over dead bodies. The lucky ones nipped around everything; the unlucky ones who got confused and slowed up: they were cut down in ambush. Basically, we used cunning to sneak through to the end of each day. No one could ask for mercy, because no one ever stopped to talk.

"Once I ran from nine to three o'clock. Hunters were chasing us toward Rukiri; we crisscrossed out there in every direction, veering, pirouetting, scrambling up and scrambling down, with never a chance to catch our breath. We knew we were racing toward death, but we wanted to dodge through life for as long as possible. Thwarted by ambushes, we would slip between them and return to Kayumba. One day we collapsed, beyond exhausted, facedown in a sorghum field. Luckily our pursuers had run out of wind, too, and had given up shortly before, without our realizing it. That day the hunt began with a hundred of us; it ended with thirty: all the others had been cut down along the way. After the genocide, it never occurred to me to run competitively in Kigali, but now I think I would have won every medal around, as far away as Nairobi or even America.

"At night, Nyamata sparkled. *Interahamwe* would drive about in small vans, waving flags and machetes as if they'd won a soccer championship. We could hear their songs and slogans as well as the music. Smoke would rise in columns from courtyards. We couldn't smell the cooking, but it had to be good. They were surely drinking Primus, eating brochettes, joking around . . . Time wasn't nipping at *their* heels. We knew they were celebrating. When they feasted, we were pleased, knowing for certain they wouldn't come up after us in the meantime. We used to say, Let them keep it up: eating, dancing, that's just great for all of us.

"We'd use the time to go down and dig up manioc, pick bananas, fix some food. It wasn't fancy cooking, since we had no salt, oil, or utensils; we ate food raw with our bare hands. We slept on leaves or bean pods. When it rained, even all night, we were delighted to have some of our filthiness rinsed off."

· · ·

Innocent: "Evenings, they were good. We felt as if we'd become savages again and we wanted to stay that way. We were almost turning into animals. We envied their happiness. We ate things without cooking them, without washing our hands: manioc lying right on the ground. We drank by licking trees. We picked off one another's lice; we scratched our scabs with fingernails so long we could pick our teeth with them. But we preferred to endure every indignity rather than die. Even to live naked all our lives rather than lose them. We saw ourselves living like monkeys.

"Once, I remember, we talked about that together, about us—how, little by little, we were changing into monkeys. Someone said that the only difference between us and the chimpanzees . . . was that no one was exterminating them. We decided, Fine, if they let us live like chimps from now on, that's okay. We'll settle without a peep for that new existence in our forest. Foraging for food, begetting our new children in the woods, making monkey faces at one another, sleeping up in the trees, making friends, poking fun at Nyamata from afar—we'll take it. We're willing to stay here for years and years, quietly, until we die a sweet, natural death. But no more running all day, no more quaking before sharpened machetes."

Eugénie: "What we weren't up to doing was fooling around with love. We shuffled off love and sex. Men, women—that fire had almost gone out among us. First of all, I think, because we weren't yet used to being so stinking and full of vermin. Also, because we felt a bit like brothers and sisters. There weren't any more males and females, if I may use that vocabulary. Death spoiled that kind of thinking. Other than that, we finally got used to our existence.

"We endured the same fate, sharing exhaustion or death, and there was nothing to fight about. Some people could become quarrelsome, bickering over sweet potatoes, for example, but they were the rare exceptions, because we all knew how surely arguments speeded up death. There were no traitors among us: the forest had no caves to hide in, so the killers never bothered trying bribery to find us. We couldn't hope to negotiate either, because who can talk while running?

"We discovered many new feelings. First off, a special kindness, and stubbornness: how not to slide into anguish or despair, and how to avoid doing things that were risky for others. People returning empty-handed from the fields might be fed by those who'd been luckier.

"We learned how to live with one another and with certain death. We learned bravery in defiance, so to speak. Those who awoke in the morning too weak to run one more day gave up on escaping, but no able-bodied person willingly waited for the machete. We almost learned how not to cry out before death. In the first days the victims wept and shouted before the fatal blow. Later on, they stopped. They no longer hoped for mercy, no longer begged to be spared; many wounded faced death without grieving aloud, except for moans of pain, of course.

"Refugees from other regions appeared in the forest after about three weeks. They had fled as best they could along rivers and through woods, crossing the Nyabarongo without trouble, bringing rumors of what was happening elsewhere. But they grumbled about the trap they now discovered in Kayumba. 'There's cutting every day in Kanombe, too,' they said, 'but at least you can escape from it, and in Nyamwiza Marsh as well, the hunters all arrive singing, but you can wait hidden in the muck, without exhausting yourself all day long.' They were so disappointed, but going back where they'd come from—that was hopeless.

"In the forest, nothing could humiliate us. Even a lady who'd torn her panties climbing over some roots, she didn't feel embarrassed. It was only afterward that shame welled up. One evening, around midnight, we tried to take the road to Cyugaro and managed to reach Nyamwiza Marsh for the last two days of the genocide. Down there the fugitives were muddy but more presentable, in better health, less worn-out, more talkative, and their clothes weren't so ragged. They had kept some babies alive, and old mamas. I felt humiliated. You could tell the marsh survivors saw us as the lowest form of life."

Innocent: "Educated people felt the most degraded. I know a teacher named Élisabeth who died of misery from crawling through the bush. During the first week we didn't think the hunts would last. The intellectuals tried to philosophize about the situation. Unlike the farmers, they craved explanations more than water itself. Some of them even jotted things down on scraps of paper before losing their Bics and notes. They kept apart from the peasants to talk among themselves; their manner was more dignified, aloof. They presented themselves somewhat as leaders, advising on the distribution of food, repeating lessons of survival learned when they were Boy Scouts, offering predictions. They spoke of Hutu colleagues and their insane plots, insisted we'd be saved by the *inkotanyi* or by foreign intervention, claimed we'd soon be allowed to go into exile abroad.

"But as the days passed, they lost credibility, because all their plans fell apart. They saw their knowledge drying up. Book learning helped us in the beginning to be patient and endure our ordeal, but later it became a liability. Philosophizing, examining history—that could hamper and discourage us. We didn't suffer from losing intellectual routines like reading or holding meetings, because we were too tormented by our fear of death. Being shunted aside was what depressed us. Self-respect deserted us at the worst moment. We'd been replaced by uneducated boys, sturdier fellows who seemed better equipped to run and forage, thanks to their former lives of hardship.

"The farmers who kept saying, 'Take no thought for the morrow,' they drew strength from that. They were bent on survival without comparing what they were going through with stories from the past about the Jews, the colonialists, or the *mwami*—our Tutsi kings. Their single-mindedness sustained them. And the longer the hunts lasted, the more important the herdsmen and smugglers became. They proved the sliest, especially in snagging food. Some even brought back chickens.

"Those boys were in great demand as group leaders, and they could freely disparage or ridicule any teachers who behaved stuffily. The time for intellectualizing was good and gone. We had to behave humbly, imitate the farmers' obsession with grubbing in the earth, and copy the tricks of illiterates."

Eugénie: "Without realizing it, we'd lost part of our minds, in a way. In the evening we talked. We knew the Hutus were busy carousing, singing, socializing, and that's when we got together. We'd speak of those left behind that day. We'd discuss what had happened. Someone would relate how somebody had died in such and such a way, or how somebody else had cleverly found a better way to escape. We'd share the misadventures of the day. We'd also whisper about our modest hopes and exchange little farewells. That soothed our souls.

"We never spoke of anything else. We never shared any memories, never—the good times of the past, never. We no longer spoke of our families, former lives, absent dear ones. All forgotten. Before—finished. Now we were all the same, sharing the same life, and that's all we talked about."

Innocent: "What did we think about during all those days? I have no answer. We were like puppets up there: we only ran, ate, rested, waited. Our intelligence was in shock. I don't remember now, I have no answer. I can't come up with anything, I don't even want to try anymore. I really can't remember if I thought at all. We were living a new existence. We were desolate, we were just stunned. It's impossible to say why no thoughts came to mind. When you get right down to it . . . we weren't alive enough for that.

"Did we recall the past? No, I'm sure not. Memories of the good old days—'I used to have ten lovely cows'*; 'my eldest son was going to take the national scholarship exam'; jokes from Alphonse's *cabaret*—no, no, I never heard the like. Perhaps one could indeed go off alone under the trees to brood, but reminisce that way in public? Never. In my opinion, it simply didn't occur to us. It was forbidden, somehow.

"In the beginning, there were moments when we mulled things over in secret. Personally, I thought about life, on the one hand; on the other, I counted the days before my end, convinced I would soon be leaving the human race, but I can't bear telling you about that now. It grieves me. It can also distress me so much

---

* Breeding Ankole cattle is the time-honored prerogative of the Tutsis, who raise them as a repository and sign of wealth rather than for human consumption. The Ankole is an ancient breed—of medium size, slender and sinewy, distinguished by splendid lyre-shaped horns and a small cervical hump similar to those of Indian cattle. The communal herds, which were almost wiped out during the genocide—either slaughtered on the spot or rounded up and driven to Congo—have rebounded to their pre-1994 numbers, thanks to the strength of this age-old tradition.

To make raising livestock more profitable (and defuse tension between Hutus and Tutsis over trampled fields), the Rwandan government is promoting the consumption of beef and milk and the restriction of formerly free-ranging herds. One consequence of this agrarian reform policy has been the recent introduction of Western cattle breeds, which now pose a serious threat to the Ankole.

that my memory breaks down. It doesn't bother me to relive life in Kayumba in my imagination, or to tell you about it, but remembering what we thought about is beyond me.

"In the evening or at night, we could take time for private moments. Myself, I'd think about my wife and son, about all we had done, about the Hutus we'd find in ambush the next morning, how to beg for mercy and promise never to be a Tutsi again if allowed to escape . . . we talked to ourselves like that. But pondering real ideas—impossible, because we no longer thought the way we had before. We mused about this and that, about one dead person after another, God, our wives. It bucked us up, steeled us against despair.

"I believe we talked to ourselves to seek someone deep inside us who could inspire courage, someone braver, more confident, who would show us that life wasn't over, that we weren't complete monkeys, that among the girls running with us, there was one with whom we might actually have children. Such private thoughts were comforting.

"Today Kayumba Forest brings me hope. I appreciate Kayumba. I myself have been up there twice, to walk among the eucalyptus, look down on the town again as we used to, seek out all our forest paths. The fear and panic have left the place; I'm not afraid of memories, or nightmares, or ghosts. I love the atmosphere of Kayumba.

"One day, during the killings, I made this firm resolution: If I make it, if I come down from this hill alive, I'll leave this region forever. I will go to Tanzania and never come back to a hill even for a visit or on business. I'll never set eyes on the homestead where I was born. I will never again meet anyone from this genocide.

"I never did leave, not really. I've even drawn quite close to the forest, since I now live in the Kayumba neighborhood of

Nyamata. And if it were possible to build a little house up there, I'd move my family in, I'd sow my small plot of land among the eucalyptus. Yes, I would live at peace in the forest. We gathered there as six thousand and finished up with twenty. That is something. I see Kayumba as the only place on earth where I could live happily ever after, because if I was not cut down in Kayumba, that was a miracle."

A SURVIVOR'S HAPPINESS

There's little chance that any guidebook to this region of Rwanda would ever mention Eugénie Kayierere's *cabaret*, off the path to Kanzenze, but the place is never empty. There's no sign, no name on the outside of this homely establishment in one of fifty identical adobe houses of a *mudugudu* without any trees or gardens offering relief from the mud or dust.

Two benches border the little courtyard outside, poorly shielded from bad weather by sheet-metal roofing pocked with holes. Set up between a small parlor and the proprietors' bedroom, the *cabaret* is a dark space furnished with a plank shelf, two more benches, and, lined up against the back wall, jerry cans and bottles sprouting "straws," tag ends of reed through which customers can sip the *urwagwa*. No one wastes money here drinking Primus or Fanta.

Eugénie spends her days in this room emptying and refilling the *urwagwa* containers or half listening to the patrons' boozy conversations. Sometimes, early in the afternoon, she shows up to sip a beer with her girlfriends at The Widows' Corner, her friend Marie-Louise's *cabaret* near the Kanzenze bus stop.

Neither her languid demeanor nor her plump silhouette gives any hint of Eugénie's phenomenal athletic performance in Kayumba Forest twelve years earlier, and even more amazingly, the cruel ordeal has left no mark upon her face. In general, most of the women survivors are remarkably cheerful, "all smiles": Marie-Louise has a kindly smile; Berthe's is mocking; Sylvie's is seductive; Francine's, vivacious . . . Between two smiles, however, their faces cloud over, and one can never tell if it's with sadness, hatred, or despair. But Eugénie's gentle face seems to radiate nothing but sweetness and joy.

Eugénie's parents moved from Kigali to the peaceful hill of Kanzenze in 1973, the year of President Habyarimana's coup d'état. The father was a mason, the mother farmed the family plot, and Eugénie went to school and helped out in the fields after class.

A pretty girl, she charmed a shopkeeper, Jean-Claude Harelimana, the owner of a retail business along the main road plus a few fertile fields near the marshes. In 1990, at the age of seventeen, she married him. Two years passed without any pregnancy; then a third, more worrisome; and then a fourth, frankly alarming. After five years, on the eve of the massacres, the couple still had no children. In the chaos of the first hunting expeditions, Eugénie and her husband were separated in the middle of the night, and she followed her fate as a fugitive to Kayumba Forest.

Today, Eugénie affirms, "If I'd had children like all Rwandan wives, I would not have survived in the forest. That curse tipped into a blessing up there, if I may say so. All the mamas were cut: all, without exception—the mamas of babies, toddlers, or older children. Because they were too slowed down by a child clinging to their hands or bundled on their backs. Me, no."

And so on the last day of the genocide, when her husband took advantage of the sudden calm to go up into the woods, Jean-Claude Harelimana found his wife still alive, and brought her down with the last few survivors to await the imminent arrival of the *inkotanyi* and the exodus of the Hutus.

Eugénie continues: "When I saw myself standing safe and sound by my husband's side, I realized something extraordinary had happened to us. For both of us to survive, in such separate places, without knowing this or seeing each other—no one else could understand what that's like . . . But I did not yet know just how extraordinary our destiny was. I reached the marshes like a filthy tramp. Later, when I went home, I felt ashamed. No more roof, no more clothes, no more relatives, no more neighbors. And no child, of course, either to raise or even to mourn. My husband had changed more than I had: the killings affected him more deeply; I could see they'd marked him in a worrisome way. I had kept some obsessions from the forest, like eating sweet potatoes without peeling them and without plates. That didn't last long—nature reminded me of my good manners—but my morale abandoned me. When I met people I knew on the paths, we asked one another who was dead and who alive; we spoke of memories and shared news of our families. I saw that people were going to rejoin life with new children, while I, with my old sorrows . . . I felt ever more desperate."

One day we sit chatting in a corner of a meadow not far from the *mudugudu*, with our bottles of beer set down next to us on the grass. Eugénie picks up her story:

"There I was, married to a man in an excellent financial situation, a fine catch. For five years no children had come along, but there was nothing I could do about it, so I bit my tongue.

"My husband tried to bear up under that, to stare down the jeering remarks, to be patient and keep his temper. He said nothing. But his family voiced their displeasure. They put it about that their lineage was going to disappear because I couldn't give him children as anticipated, that the bride-price had gone for nothing. They suspected me, they accused me, and I was too humiliated to be scared. They pointed out other girls who'd gotten married in the same year and were bearing children properly. I was so, so discouraged. Reason why, when I felt the first discomforts of pregnancy, I was pessimistic. But when the warnings kept coming favorably, then I understood that extraordinary omen."

Through what mystery of maternity, what metabolic upheaval, does Eugénie give birth to a baby ten months after her return from Kayumba? Within a year a second infant arrives, followed as quickly as they can by four brothers and sisters in that house in the *mudugudu*. More are expected.

"Not having any children," says the mama, "is traumatic for a Rwandan woman. Yet, in my case, luck saved my life in Kayumba and then allowed me to bring fresh life into this world. The genocide simplified happiness for me, by which I mean the children. Still, I do know that I must not ordinarily say such things, out of respect for the departed."

A LITTLE GIRL IN THE
WRONG COLUMN

At lunch that day, a promise of delights: chicken marinated in milk and grilled with tomatoes over a wood fire as only Marie-Louise and Janvière, her cook, can prepare it. With a side dish of creamy puréed beans and bananas, of course. One guest whom I have not yet met is already sitting at the table: a tall, stout lady who speaks a lovely Congolese French and has been smiling ever since she arrived. Marie-Louise gestures toward her.

"May I present Médiatrice, who has just received her secondary-school diploma in the humanities. She's waiting for the grades to be posted to know where she will continue her studies."

"Oh, really! Bravo! What would you like to study?"

"Everything suits me. Why not medicine, or literature? The choice will depend solely on the grade rankings."

"Aren't you going to ask her why she's graduating from school at her age?" prompts Marie-Louise.

"Yes, of course . . ." I take the bull by the horns: "I suppose the genocide interrupted your education . . ."

"Not at all!" exclaims Marie-Louise, laughing. "It's because she got lost in a forest."

"During all this time? What forest? You don't mean Kayumba, do you?"

"Kayumba at the very beginning," replies Médiatrice. "Then the dark equatorial rain forest."

At that moment, I realize she is the little girl about whom Eugénie and Innocent had told me, and I think of those stories of Japanese soldiers who disappeared into the jungles of Pacific islands at the end of the Second World War and were found fifteen or twenty years later, wandering among the trees, ignorant of Japan's surrender and the peace. Unbelievable stories.

"I was born in the hamlet of Mayange; we were three brothers and three sisters. I was much spoiled by my papa because I was his favorite. My parents farmed in the early morning; an apprentice herdsman watched the cows, and we drank our fill of milk. There was also a flourishing banana plantation, and when my parents finished a new batch of *urwagwa*, they shared with the neighboring families; that was the ambience. We lived in a sheet-metal adobe, the typical house of the Bugesera. The children were neat and clean: Mama took great care of us. She was smart, because she'd gone to school, and she made us do lessons in mathematics and French, especially vocabulary.

"Papa had fled the massacres of Ruhengeri in 1959. He started out as a small vendor in the marketplace, where Mama came to shop, and that's how they took a liking to each other. Mama's family intervened against the marriage, but Papa bested them all to win her.

"So, as it's done here, Papa set up Mama on his land in Mayange. Papa was a jovial guy, somewhat imposing, quite tall, who was kind and cordial with the neighbors. He worked a lot, and apart from a few setbacks made good headway in business. Mama was amiable, fat, of a reddish complexion, and loved to laugh with everyone.

"We'd gotten used to that wonderful life. Nothing bothered us, save for a little segregation in school, when the teacher asked us each our ethnicity, but that wasn't serious. We lived next to the Hutus with no gestures of ill will.

"I felt the first danger in 1992, when we were driven from the house in Mayange. They slaughtered the cows, burned the surrounding homes, and Papa moved us to one of his houses in Nyamata. For us children, life returned to normal: we went to school, we played. Our parents went mornings to the land in Mayange to bring back food. Mama had changed, though: She felt deprived and victimized; she was no longer that laughing lady. She tried to tell us little tales or give us math problems to do, but her voice had lost some of its joy. Whenever Papa came home from the *cabaret*, he'd tell us again how he'd been threatened in Ruhengeri, with the burnings and suchlike killings.

"April 6, that was the crash of Habyarimana's plane. At noon on April 11, soldiers streamed toward the marketplace and began shooting. Papa left with some children for the church, thinking it would be quiet there, as it had been in the churches in Ruhengeri. I missed their departure, though, and followed one of my big sisters. We hid in a shopkeeper's house, where all day long we heard the screams of the wounded left to die. That evening we decided to go up to Kayumba Forest. As we ran we saw bodies lying around; we had never seen death before, so we yelled, 'Wake up, run away like us!'

"Up there, a kind of hide-and-seek awaited us, as Eugénie has already told you, I believe. I handled myself very well in the melee, but since I was a little girl, I ran behind. Even if you count one by one each evening we stayed alive, those days in Kayumba count more than years, as much as an eternity.

"One day we were caught in an ambush, and there my legs refused to move. Luckily, the attackers chose to follow the group of women without lingering to cut me. I lost track of my big sister and found myself too alone, quite desolate. I thought about the gruesome death stalking me. I was a lost little girl, and I decided to go back down to Nyamata; even if I wound up butchered like the others, I still longed to see my mama or papa.

"In our courtyard, I met a Hutu woman named Fortunée who rented a house from my father. She gave me a sweet potato and she hid me. I spent my days hearing the shouts and songs. The *interahamwe* would ask if I wasn't Tutsi, and the kind lady would answer no.

"When the gunshots of the *inkotanyi* rang out in Kayumba, everyone decided to flee. Oh, I was very scared among all those Hutus. They whipped up chaos, the streets were in an uproar. The lady told me, 'If you stay, since you know you're Tutsi, a passing killer will surely guess and cut you in anger before fleeing himself. Come along behind the Hutu column.' I followed a family down the road, but they drove me away, so I followed another. With the stubbornness of childhood I walked alone in the rear. Kids made friends along the way; we ate in abandoned fields, slept back to back on leaves. From Kibuye we went by pirogue on Lake Kivu all the way to Congo.

"One morning I was suspected of being Tutsi. Some children from our primary school had given me away. I was surrounded by a small crowd that questioned me, demanding my papa's name. They decided to kill me and took me with a big fuss before an *interahamwe*, an expert in cutting. 'You mosquito,' he exclaimed, 'you're the one they want me to cut? I thought you'd be bigger!' He had a good laugh and gave me a hundred francs from his pocket to buy bananas. Then a family claimed me right away. I believe they were willing because they realized I'd bring in small change for doing household chores.

"Later on, Congolese women typically came looking for orphans to work in their homes. I was picked up by a Mama Giroud in Giziza. I lasted two years as a *boyeste*, a girl 'servant boy,' but she was a mama of good heart who let me share the plate with her children.

"The *inkotanyi* attacks began in September 1996, and they drove me to the refugee camp. We were really pounded. One night the shelling was awful, with bodies everywhere, people jumping straight into the lake, and the panic scattered us. I high-tailed it into the tall trees. I saw heaps of corpses all along the path. I followed a lady named Marie, and we found a column of fugitives. We had no idea that most of those behind us would be taken home in good health to Rwanda. And that's how I fled into the great equatorial rain forest.

"It was a shadowy and scary place, not easy to describe. Giant trees hid the sky; vines imprisoned the paths; scavengers like hyenas preyed on the bodies of the unlucky. Many birdcalls and cries, many big snakes of different colors. Chimpanzees, macaques, howling monkeys day and night. But the forest animals seemed rested, well nourished, and we could see they weren't aggressive—except for the baboons, of course, who'd attack any women who had a strong smell. We reached the territory of the Batembo, a most wicked tribe that killed us in great numbers. *Interahamwe* or former soldiers were our scouts, but the column was disorganized, because even our leaders could not find their bearings in the darkness under the tall trees. The march to Rangi lasted a year. We spent the next year resting in a small camp until we were pushed out. Then we marched through Wakilele, Bakili, Nakele, Masisi.

"We ate fruit from wild trees, and some poor folks died from bad fruit or sickness or exhaustion. We walked blindly, just kept going. We walked to keep from stopping. We could go along together for several weeks, then take fright and disperse in all directions. Deep down, we didn't care where we went: it depended on chance, and the attacks.

"We were blocked by RPF [Rwandan Patriotic Front] soldiers, who could turn murderous. We were driven on by the fearsome *interahamwe*. The two groups were at each other's throats—no point in picking between them. If you weren't lucky enough to be captured alive, you had to run away. The Mai Mai militias,* the Batembo and Bayenga tribes, the *interahamwe*—for any of them, anywhere, we were zeros in rags, walking target practice. I've seen thousands of dead. Fatigue, sickness, poison, and weapons took their relentless toll on us.

"In the forest, we behaved like crazy people: we saw ghosts, we heard dead souls come back to chastise us, we ran from them, we feared the spirits would attack us, we protected our ears from their mystical screams. Some of us listened to them and went off with the spirits, never to return. We'd build shelters of foliage, completely unlike those of humans. When we broke camp, we'd just build new ones later. It was a treacherous, almost animal existence.

"Along the way, I never spoke of my childhood, never pronounced the word *Tutsi*, because if the family helping me had suspected the truth, they would have cut me. Between two

---

* *Initially formed to defend local territories in Congo—first against Tutsi forces that invaded in pursuit of Hutu* interahamwe *and against the RPF's Congolese rebel allies—various Mai Mai militia groups are still active today, mostly in the eastern Kivu provinces. Savage warlords, bandits, and guerrillas have devastated Congo for years, preying particularly on women. Each armed group has a trademark style of rape as a weapon of war; the Mai Mai rape with branches and bayonets, mutilating their victims, often leaving them crippled, sterile, incontinent, infected with HIV, and outcasts in their own country. —Translator's note*

deaths, I had to choose the lesser, and that was hanging on as a Hutu with Hutus.

"With the passing years, there were fewer hunts. I came to a stop in the Masisi region. I was taken by a family in Niarunza, in the south of the country; the plantations there seemed prosperous, and I could eat my fill of mangoes and coconuts. It was in 2001 that I heard voices in agreement, warbling about calm in Rwanda, especially for the Tutsis, and I began longing to go back. The family insisted it was still risky. On the sly, I negotiated a trip home with a Congolese called Papa Chance. I farmed a double load to raise the money. We set out. Halfway there, we encountered Red Cross trucks in Novombo. For one week I waited with some companions in exile without uttering a word. The relief workers handed out blankets, flour, forms to fill in, and loaded us into the backs of the trucks. They dropped me off on the banks of the Nyabarongo.

"I thought Wednesday would be a good time to return to Nyamata, because it was market day. March 13, 2002. I went knocking on the door at home; strangers lived there, selling *urwagwa*. They told me a lady had already laid a claim to the house, and I thought, Maybe a sister.

"Nyamata had changed. The day I fled, the houses were burning, the sheet metal had been stripped. Now the houses seemed normal again, but all the people looked like strangers.

"I went to the district office. My uncle was summoned and didn't recognize me. When people began telling me about everyone I knew who had died, I wept for the first time, because I knew almost nothing about the quick and the dead. I went back to our land in Mayange. I felt guilty for following the Hutus in that long flight, which I didn't dare recount to relieve my distress for fear of sparking contempt or suspicion. Afterward, I decided to live with Dorothée, one of my older sisters, in Nyamata.

"When I'd gone away in 1994, I'd completed three years in primary school, and shame sat on the bench with me in fourth grade. The pupils made fun of me in class: 'Here's the fat lady back from Congo!' I went to a big brother's house, where he taught me to conjugate verbs and do math problems. One teacher, who liked me for asking so many questions, would wait for me when the subject was tricky, and schooling came back to me. Today, I'm fine, and have just completed my humanities, as you know.

"The struggles that go on in my head between the memories from before and after my flight drive me to tears. Whenever I'm at a loss in some way, I despair. I'm frightened of war, all wars, even far-off ones, even on television. Everyone living in Rwanda in '94 knows the curse of war in Africa. I'm happy to be African. I love African songs, from Rwanda and Congo alike. I believe that Africans are the nicest people in the world. But they are greedy among themselves. It isn't the Whites who blow on the glowing coals of massacres: no White raised a machete in Nyamata or forced a Hutu to raise his. It was envy, and fear of poverty. Africans are born with both a special kindness and a special wickedness inside. When there's a party, all the neighbors are invited; let a misunderstanding arise, and those very guests whip out their machetes and burn down houses. They turn greedy, mean, throwing away their civilization, thinking only of their tribe—reason why they are banished from the modern world.

"Ethnicity—I certainly know something about that now. Being Tutsi, being Hutu, they're not the same. The Hutu is the Tutsi's most dangerous enemy. That's my first thought whenever I go to my land in Mayange. Memory keeps everything, and the most painful memories are right on top. In Congo, I studied ethnic wickedness, and I also learned to live with absolutely anyone, to be dignified in misfortune, to eat raw food without salt. I got used to wearing rags over my scabbed and dirty skin, to get by with nothing, to endure the hard labor of a field *boyeste*, to wander in a dark forest full of nasty monkeys.

"I spent eight years compelled to say nothing about my Tutsi origins, nothing about my family, nothing about my childhood, nothing about my deepest thoughts—nothing about *me*. Eight years of living alone, always alone, without ever daring to cry from loneliness, without any chance to call someone I loved by name. There were days when I felt so abandoned that I tried to talk to myself. I used to go off into a little corner and call my own name, softly, gently. I would search for a first word . . . but I had nothing to say to myself.

"I was eleven when I fled from Nyamata, nineteen at my return. Childhood had abandoned me; adolescence wanted nothing to do with me. I missed my mama, papa, brothers, and sisters. The school songs had slipped away, and the games, the flirtations, the pretty clothes, the children's parties. My mind won't let go of a single memory. I lost a first life that was promised to me. But I feel calm, and strong, and encouraged to go after a second life. I believe in promises. Oh, no: if a blessing happens along, I'm not going to turn my back on it! In spite of everything, God watches over us; the burden eases, good fortune can come my way. Happiness is living cheerfully, surrounded by a peaceful family."

ON MAIN STREET

Always practical, Médiatrice wants to take advantage of the first afternoon of her vacation to buy school supplies. So she heads for Nyamata's main street to shop in one of the two new stationery stores in town.

It's market day. Instead of the usual small vans parked in front of Chez Rose (the big *cabaret* with its new name, Gaçaça, painted on the facade), there are double-cabin pickup trucks and air-conditioned all-terrain vehicles, beside which people from Kigali stand chatting. There's no one easier to spot in the Rwandan countryside than a Kigalois: Congolese coiffure, teetering high heels, garish makeup smeared with dust, or dark suit and tie despite the stifling heat. Throughout the world, people who live in a nation's capital enjoy cultivating their elitism, but in no other country do they take such care to avoid the slightest risk of confusion between themselves and the provincial folks they're visiting. Probably because citizens of Kigali, most of whom once belonged to the Tutsi diaspora, cannot overcome the uneasiness they have felt since their return to Rwanda after the genocide, the malaise over the impossibility of accepting a blood-drenched past that belongs to them yet is not theirs.

Entering Rose's place, you walk past a bar over which Rose herself presides. She is an Anglophone who once spent a long time in exile off in Nairobi and now keeps track of her accounts with an air of typically Kenyan distinction. At the far end of the bar, you step out into a vast circular veranda open on all sides, surrounded by a series of green-walled little "salons."

Today that veranda is indisputably the domain of the region's military governor, who sits among his officers nursing a beer. A White (quite rare in the Bugesera), the French manager of the waterworks, is relaxing with his foremen at a neighboring table. The waterworks was built by a French company, and it comes on the heels of a road constructed by a German concern, which follows the installation of electrical cables and telephone lines financed by the European Union, and a hospital set up by a Pentecostal church. The marshes are due to be drained, but in the meantime there is also a plan for a new marketplace and perhaps a new and improved soccer field. Like the rest of Rwanda, Nyamata is attracting manna from a compassionate or guilt-ridden West without, however, understanding the risks of such dependence.

Across from Chez Rose, on the other side of the main street, the market held on Wednesdays and Saturdays is bustling, proof that Hutus are no longer reluctant to shop here. The merchants of Nyamata claim the market is nothing compared to what it was years past, when people came from a hundred kilometers around. That is true of the ambience, perhaps, but not of the activity. Every bit of ground is in use on the esplanade, where wholesalers, women farmers, and craftsmen respect a mysterious corporatist geography, as in all marketplaces of Africa. Off to the left, you find vegetables, bananas, manioc, beans. Close by on the right, shoes. In the middle, clothing and fabrics; here, poultry; there, fish, various kinds of flour, old radios, and batteries both new and used. The vendors of goats and charcoal have moved to the old soccer field, near which a rummage sale of mats and crockery has reappeared.

Among the less attractive changes, I might mention the portraits of the president of the republic on the once vividly colored umbrellas that shade farm wives, or young women concerned about their complexions, or babies carried on their mamas' backs; the small mountains of plastic flip-flops of a thickness as disgraceful as their fluorescent colors; black backpacks, a true aesthetic disaster; and, finally, heaps of what is called "secondhand"— Western clothing acquired through who knows what traffic in charitable donations and resold at laughably low prices that threaten the livelihood of local dealers in fabrics and apparel.

Fortunately, at this writing, the piecework seamstresses are still on the job behind their Singers or Butterflys, big black sewing machines with gilt ornamentation. They toil side by side next to the displays of fabric, while well-known couturières who make suits and trousers to measure are more comfortably installed in nearby workshops. Jeannette's spot is empty. Seeing my surprised dismay, her colleagues laugh: "Don't worry! Mademoiselle Jeannette gave birth at last this morning, but she'll surely be back at work on Saturday."

Passing on news of survivors, following their adventures, means continuing to talk about the genocide. In the case of Jeannette Ayinkamiye, it would mean launching into endless installments, so greatly does the genocide still disrupt her everyday life.

At our first meeting years ago, Jeannette was a teenage farmer who had this to say to me: "Someone who has seen atrocious suffering for so long can never again live among others as before, because this person will remain on guard, suspicious of people, even if they have done nothing." After her father and brothers were killed during the terrible events of 1994, Jeannette had fled with her mother and sisters into the marshes, where Hutu *interahamwe* seriously wounded her little sisters and chopped off her mother's arms and legs, leaving her to die in the mud. In answer to questions from readers of *Life Laid Bare*, I have often repeated something else Jeannette said to me: "I don't believe those who say that we have seen the worst of atrocities for the last time. When a genocide has been committed, another one can come, no matter when, no matter where, in Rwanda or anyplace, if the root cause is still there and still unknown."

Two years ago I had left Jeannette in Kanazi, where she had found refuge in a pretty little fired-brick house lent to her by a humanitarian organization. By hiring herself out in the fields, she was feeding a swarm of orphans. What had she been up to since then?

"Ever since the killings I've been unlucky," she told me. "Life has turned toward the past, and my thoughts waver when I bump into failures. For example, when I *get*, I grab hold, but I'm forced to let go when I stumble over discouragements."

Such as? "I don't like to detail them. That worries me. That makes me afraid."

Without going into all her ups and downs, here is the gist of her story: "Drought was baking the earth, the hoe was too heavy for me . . . I had to feed too many children I had not borne. No candidate was ever going to present himself to lend a hand. I left farming . . . I bought spices at a bazaar and tried peddling them in the marketplace . . . A certain Anastase rented me a sewing machine on her veranda. I liked sewing things. I did earn some small change, but the drought turned customers away . . . I signed on as a wholesale dealer in the shop of a charity association for needy women; I sold sugar, rice, and oil. Since no one paid, that didn't work, and I had to leave; I didn't even put the padlock on the door . . . A radio announcement said the local defense forces were hiring recruits; eager for the salary, I tried to wear the uniform, but the training threatened me with exhaustion, so I gave up . . . The association for needy women complained to the police about wastage in their shop. I was judged responsible for the problem, but I couldn't pay anything back, so I ran away into the hills to hide; I was caught, I spent days in prison . . . Someone stole my sewing machine one night. My little sister died of poison in her belly . . . There you have it.

"Luckily, after that, time pushed me forward again. I am going from less to better, I don't feel cursed anymore . . . A new machine was bought for me. Life continues to offer complications; still, it offers acts of Providence as well. His name is Sylvestre Bizimana. He drives a pedicab. He picked me up as a customer on several evenings and brought me back to Kanazi after my sewing work at the market . . . We came to an understanding . . . The pregnancy happened . . . He seemed very affectionate . . . We'll get married when we've saved up a bit for expenses, because he rents his pedicab. The humanitarian organization put me out of the fired-brick house because I'm not an orphan anymore and got myself pregnant . . . I live in a sheet-metal adobe in Gatare . . . Debts come rushing in, difficulties stand in line for us, but we have enough sorghum porridge to eat . . . Heaven has chosen me to be a mother: I finally had my child, and that's a very big thing."

In Nyamata, only the lively colors of the fabrics on display—red, blue, yellow, green—lend a hint of exuberance to the streets. Rwanda is in fact a land of halftones; it's also a place of gentle sounds and mellow flavors. Its cuisine is not as highly spiced as in the rest of Africa. The music is almost as sentimental as the Portuguese fado, and the liturgical choral singing, very classical and melodic, never becomes emotional. Rwanda is called the land of a thousand hills, not to emphasize any diversity multiplied by a thousand, but to make clear that a thousand hills in a small territory leave no room for deserts, high plateaus, virgin forests, spectacular landscapes. Even Burundi, Rwanda's neighbor and almost its twin, breathes with the vast open waters of Lake Tanganyika and resounds with the drumming of its traditional orchestras.

Rwanda is also the land of confabs and secret meetings. In a Rwandan *cabaret*, what do two men do when they want to have a brief private chat? They stand up, go off to one side, hold hands, whisper for a moment, then come sit down again as naturally as you please. If two women are quarreling, one of them sends a neighbor as a go-between to resolve the problem quietly. When people bargain over a harvest, a job, some kind of collaboration, they do so without palaver, taking no pleasure in traditions of haggling: terms are negotiated crisply and the handshake is swift. "Hush-hush," the famous rumors of the hills, fuels many a conversation; poisonings, which are legendary, belong to this cult of secretiveness. Most people eat at home, shielded from nosy neighbors, and invite others to join them only on ceremonial occasions. A family's cows are hidden in the anonymity of a herd, watched over in the bush by a guardian dressed in rags that help protect his charges from envious eyes. Men hide their mistresses. Polite greetings and modest embraces respect highly coded rituals. People speak in soft, almost uninflected voices, and they speak Kinyarwanda, a concise language with an incredibly sophisticated grammar, a tongue shared only with Burundi and impermeable to Swahili, French, and English.

The shyness of the people and the quiet subtlety of the landscapes surprise those who learned of Rwanda through the unspeakable brutality of the genocidal massacres in 1994. Mainstreet buildings are discreet: there are no garish signs, no eye-catching poetic or comical advertisements to spark your interest, no mind-blowing murals or painted truck decorations like those found in any other city of the African Great Lakes region, as in

Zanzibar, Kampala, Kinshasa, or farther away in Kano or Oua-gadougou. The facades painted green—every shade of green: eucalyptus, coffee-tree, or banana-plant green—or in the ocher, brown, and reddish tones of the countryside are a gentle pastel feast for the eyes.

What's new on the long kilometer of Nyamata's main street—wide enough for truck and van traffic, bikes, strolling pedestrians, and plodding herds, where the town is at its liveliest? Many new pharmacies attest to the good health of the medical professions. Marking a timid upswing in local business activity, still more tiny bank offices are offering microloans, the latest World Bank and UN initiative in vogue, one that smacks of both humanitarianism and usury.

It is the dry season, and there are too many millers waiting for customers in front of their electric mills. Bakery-cafeterias offer only one kind of bread and fritters, and curiously identical cakes. It's impossible, for example, to convince Sylvie, who has opened a bakery looking out onto an agreeable veranda at the main inter-section, to ask Gaspard, her talented assistant, to bake other doughs, to try out other kinds or flavors of breads and cakes.

Pedicabs, above all, have multiplied, but without losing their elegance, with their heavy black frames, chrome hubcaps and three or four shiny rearview mirrors, passenger seats of black-fringed red or blue leather. There are also, as in Kigali, a few lux-urious moped- and motorbike-taxis. Across from the minibus stop, there's a taxi stand at the entrance to Main Street, but the most important one is still in the shade of a massive acacia tree at the main intersection, near Chicago's beer warehouse. A third stand, at the far end of the street, points the way to Kanazi and—farther along—N'genda. Beginning at dawn, bicyclists pedal nonstop to carry passengers, animals, or beans (up to five twenty-five-kilo bags tied to the rear wheel). These men cover Nyamata and the surrounding area sometimes late into the night, when they fetch back the last drinkers, often dozens of kilometers away, along rocky and ravine-furrowed slopes that would annihilate the most stalwart competitor in the Tour de France, even one on steroids.

On market days, if you park yourself on a bench beneath an awning—in front of Théoneste's shop, for example, where he's always good for a chuckle—you'll get the impression that everyone you know on the fourteen hills will show up any minute now. See, over there, that's Angélique Mukamanzi, holding her little Cédric's hand. She's the one who escaped the massacre in the church at nearby Ntarama, joined a band of orphans in the marshes, and afterward, with her sole surviving sister, helped care for eight of them. After going through a painful period when her face puffed up, she's slender and coquettish once again, thanks to meeting her lieutenant, no doubt. A little way back is Christine Nyiransabimana: you'd spot her a hundred meters away thanks to that laughing face she shows the whole world: she fairly radiates good humor, though as a half-Hutu, half-Tutsi woman whose Tutsi father was killed, who was herself raped and suffered greatly during her exile in Congo, she at first felt "deeply ashamed to be seen as Hutu" when she returned to Nyamata. She's pregnant with her fourth, by a staff sergeant.

Jean-Baptiste Munyankore swings by on his black bike, with the proud bearing of a smart cavalier. He pedals slowly and evenly, shoulders back and spine straight, gripping the handlebars firmly and impassively even though he has covered the fifteen kilometers from Ntarama, and through forest for half the way. He's wearing his green suit (the newest one), an embroidered shirt, his gold-rimmed glasses, and a snap-brimmed fedora. Nothing can keep him from coming, especially since his retirement after fifty-five years of teaching at the primary school in Cyugaro.

As on every market day, at dawn he accompanied his wife Bellancile to their field, where he left her, hoe in hand. He gave instructions to the boy herding their livestock, returned to the house, put on his jacket—slipping a Bic pen and a notebook into a pocket—and set out on his bike.

After his first wife died in the marshes along with nine of his eleven children, Jean-Baptiste suffered deeply from loneliness until he went looking for another mate. "I lasted only three years, because no one can go on living without a wife for help with the house, especially for food and cleaning," he explained during our last visit to his home. "Actually, alone . . . I saw myself counted out. In any case, luck was on my side: I hired a matchmaker, who sent out attractive offers. It didn't take long to find someone, and we were married without any problems." Five years later, the two surviving children he had with his first wife, now grown, have three new half brothers and sisters: Diogène, Jean, and Jeanne-d'Arc. They probably won't be the last, admits Jean-Baptiste, and this may "make complications for the family fields, because my wife is quite young and fertile."

For the moment, Jean-Baptiste wings past on his bicycle, intent on picking up his pension from the school district secretary. Then he's expected at an introductory meeting on post-traumatic stress disorders, to be held at the church with some Italian therapists. Next he has a condolence visit to make to a fellow teacher, after which he must search carefully through the goat market for a promising young black she-goat, the theft of which a few weeks ago still enrages him whenever he thinks of it. His schedule leaves most of his time free for chance encounters, however, since all his years of teaching in the primary school have released into the world whole generations of former pupils, most of whom are grateful and happy to buy him a beer.

· · ·

As though they were hurrying to a wedding, the Kibungo gang rushes past on a pack of bikes, wearing their Sunday best. Pio, in a black suit, is taking his wife, Josiane, to the health clinic for a sonogram; we'll be talking about them later on, because their marriage presents quite a mystery. Pancrace, sporting his midnight-blue satin shirt, is giving a ride to his sister, who's going to purchase some vermifuge powder for their mother. Fulgence rides solo in his white sandals, wearing a huge silver-plated crucifix around his neck and lugging two sacks of grain to sell at the marketplace, where his wife is waiting for him.

None of the gang will go to any side-street *cabaret*, because they're still afraid of provoking arguments or an altercation. *Urwagwa* is something they drink at home, on evenings up on the hill, but they'll spend the afternoon in town, strolling and chatting with friends. Three years ago, after their release, they would never have dared come down to Nyamata or amble up Main Street . . . and besides, three years ago, they didn't have any bikes or nice clothes.

WHAT DO YOU SAY?

The difficulty or even impossibility of speaking to others about one's experience, of sharing it with someone who did not live through it, is a distinguishing—and very disturbing—characteristic of the protagonists of a genocide, and it differentiates their behavior from that, more familiar to us, of people who have been through other human catastrophes (wars, ethnic cleansings, military occupations) or natural calamities (earthquakes, volcanic eruptions, droughts).

In the aftermath of those tragedies, whatever the extent of the losses and the barbaric cruelty they have revealed, survivors tend spontaneously to bear witness, often vehemently, and to relate as much as possible about what they have just endured. Palestinian kids, Sierra Leonean men, Bosnian, Chechen, or Sri Lankan women accuse, denounce, demand, point fingers, brandish fists. Such men and women protest, lament, insist, and constantly appeal to foreigners.

After a genocide, survivors and criminals alike usually keep quiet, reluctant to speak of their still-raw experience of human extermination. They sometimes share that temptation of mutism forever: the criminals, for understandable motives; the survivors, for more complex, very moving reasons. No one has forgotten the shock of the revelations during Adolf Eichmann's trial or how after years of silence Simone Veil, a French lawyer and former cabinet minister, suddenly began during an interview to describe her deportation to Auschwitz. And everyone knows that secrets may last forever in countless families, Jewish or not, where they place a crushing weight on everyone's life.

What should we think about the difficulties in speaking of such matters to a next-door neighbor, a former colleague, a once–best friend, never mind to a stranger? What about the killer face to face with a survivor, or with his own friends, his own children? Or a survivor coming face to face with the killer who murdered her family? What can you say to the person who chased you, or whom you chased, with a machete, or the person who abandoned and betrayed you? What can you say when a Rwandan fate, unique in contemporary history, requires the families of victims and the families of killers, leaders, and architects of the genocide to resume living side by side *immediately* . . . when that destiny compels them, in an overpopulated region, to take up the same roles in the same places as before—in adjoining fields, on church pews, walking along the same forest paths to market, waiting impatiently together in line at the hospital, cheering a goal from the sidelines of the Nyamata soccer field, working for one another? How do they face the vital obligation to *talk to one another*? What do you say? How do you discuss what you now share: that almost completely successful attempt at extermination?

Ignace Rukiramacumu: "Myself, I remember every detail in spite of my great age. Frankly, the killer sweeps away his memories when he knows he has failed, but he cannot kill them. He lies, that's natural, but he mustn't overdo it. Getting stuck in your own lies is risky, because time can make you believe in them, and that rots your mind. Someone who accepts a little bit of truth unloads his memory. He replaces bad memories with good, and that's beneficial.

"But the real truth isn't something you can peddle. Convincing a Tutsi you are telling the truth is impossible. Even if all the details of a situation are offered up to him, he is not persuaded: it's not possible to come to an understanding about something so serious. You try to tell how you killed a relative; he gets angry. You dodge a question; he gets equally angry and suspects you.

"We cannot talk directly about the killings, because if you reveal a wounding detail, that can be shocking for the survivor or risky for the killer. We do talk about them, but we dance around, we make false moves, we exchange shallow words. The Hutu shows himself fearful of the Tutsi because of his misdeeds, the Tutsi shows himself worried about the authorities. Nobody dares use truthful words anymore, words of evil or vengeance."

Alphonse Hitiyaremye: "We often get together, we members of the Kibungo gang: Pancrace, Pio, Ignace, Fulgence . . . We visit one another, share drinks and memories. Among ourselves, we feel at ease talking over this or that event in the marshes or in Congo. We enjoy revisiting good and bad moments together. With the Tutsis, though, we feel ill at ease.

"The thing is, the Tutsis know less than the killers about what happened, because they themselves were always scared or running away. Today they ask for details of the killings. At the first words, they get angry! Then they calm down and want to hear new information. We toss out some more, but the real truth, the atmosphere, if I may say so, cannot be told.

"Telling how we lived it so zestfully, how hot we were—no. How we cracked jokes while out hunting, how we had a Primus all around on good days, slaughtered the cows, sang in the marshes, how we casually gang-raped unlucky girls and women, how we had contests in the evenings over who had cut the most victims, or made fun of the dying in their agony and all suchlike amusements—that doesn't bear telling. Saying that everyone joined in except for a few old guys, ladies, and their tiny children—that's another truth that must be filtered.

"Once in a while, in a *cabaret*, you can run into a Tutsi who'll needle you. He's going to shoot jokes at you about how you ate his cows or stuff like that. You must take great care: if there's a little slipup, things can turn serious in no time.

"We made too many mistakes on our hunting expeditions. It's hard, now, to balance the harm we did and harm we can do by telling about it. Talking in a Tutsi family, it's confusion: no one can speak properly, you must avoid that. I prefer to recall things in a *cabaret*. You offer a bottle with good intentions, you exchange compliments, you propose lending a hand during the harvests, and underneath that is a way of talking it all over."

Pancrace Hakizamungili: "When we got out of prison, we were sent to the camp in Bicumbi. We lived three months in shelters draped with 'sheeting,' nicely set up, and we could buy *urwagwa*. The first month we heard lectures, I wrote down in a notebook with a Bic. They fed us the history of Rwanda, the succession of kings, colonists, and republics. Everything was new to me—except the genocide, of course.

"They taught us how to behave with humility and understanding on the hill. There were restless Hutus who were still disruptive on the class bench, but firm scolding corrected them. They told us: 'You left your hills with the faces of killers; you must absolutely return with the faces of lambs. You will meet rageful or vindictive Tutsis. You will encounter neighbors who know of your wrongdoing; the traumatized among them can be unpredictable. If they spit bitter words at you, don't open your mouth, turn away, appeal to someone trustworthy for help, the local authorities, for example, or simply go away.'

"They taught us to bear the difficult life that was holding out its arms to us: the droughts, sobriety, patience with the survivors. They taught us never to speak directly of the killings, never to offer appalling details. Not to offer apologies personally except before the audience at *gaçaça* gatherings. To avoid being boastful or sneering. Or even chatty. Very useful lessons on behavior."

Fulgence Bunani: "In 1994 we'd separated from the Tutsis with hateful words. We wanted no more of their frightened greetings. We called them cockroaches and the like in the *cabaret*, cackling over their approaching end. During the killings we sang savage songs, disguised ourselves as devils with headdresses of leaves, raised blood-streaked machetes, screamed insults at them, made fun of their pleas for mercy.

"Now we are talking: 'How are you, are things going well, how's the family, how's it going in the fields?' . . . We chat about the harvest; we don't use bad language. We show ourselves welcoming in both camps. The survivors appear quite surprised by our pleasant words. It's normal to change when things have not gone well."

Consolée Murekatete, the wife of Alphonse Hitiyaremye: "Women brew up more rancor and more compassion than men. Men can explode at one another with insults, whereas women— Rwandan women, in any case—must hide this among themselves, but we whisper such things every day.

"And Hutu women do this ten times more than Tutsi women. Certain among us accept the misdeeds of our husbands. They even accuse them of going wrong in the marshes, of spoiling their earlier good fortune, of cutting down good neighbors.

But other wives accept nothing. They deny everything. They even contradict their husbands' confessions. They chew over their losses. In their courtyards they murmur of vengeance so as to spoil the new understandings among women of goodwill."

Marie-Louise Kagoyire: "Whenever I speak to a Hutu, I try to camouflage what I feel—which is to say, my bad thoughts. If we are talking about work, we can easily discuss the schedule. If he needs me or I need him, fine. You can evoke the killings in a conversation, but only in the form of pleasantries, rote words, nothing substantial.

"Me, I'm not familiar with the details I would need to know about the killings. I must be careful, however: Conversation with a Hutu is a delicate thing. If I say something big, if I speak wounding words, he will feel offended, turn his back on me, and I'll find myself the loser. Frankly, one feels uneasy listening to a killer's words if he is lying, and one feels just as uneasy if he's telling the truth. As for him, he will feel ashamed of what he is saying if it's the truth, yet will be equally ashamed of his lies.

"Before, when I was little, even in poverty we felt quite respectable being Tutsi. We lived that as a mark of favor. After, we felt betrayed: threatened, humiliated, hunted. We felt guilty for being Tutsi. A curse. Now I no longer feel either shame or fear; on the contrary, I'm very, very proud of being Tutsi. I am honored to have had Tutsi parents, to have been married to a handsome Tutsi husband. To be looked at as a Tutsi. Of course I cannot say this out loud."

Cassius Niyonsaba: "The harsh politics of reconciliation forbid survivors to speak in any fashion about the killings, except when invited to give evidence, during ceremonies, mourning periods, or the *gaçaça* trials. For example, I mustn't ever say in public that

I will never marry a Hutu wife. Separatists are threatened with punishment.

"Humanitarian foundations set up training sessions so that Tutsis and Hutus learn how to talk together properly. These organizations spend millions of dollars urging us to forgive one another and make friends. But the survivors, they don't want to trade their good word for petty compensations—reason why those groups get nowhere. The survivors don't want to have anything to do with that.

"Among us survivors, we do talk about it, but with others it's impossible. Even with a foreigner, nothing is certain: there are some who might understand, but others can be mocking or aggressive. Instead of risking such defeats, it's better to close up your heart.

"Some Hutus behave nicely because they feel ashamed, but others speak on the sly about starting it up again. Some Tutsis murmur words of vengeance. If lips repeated what the heart is whispering, they would sow panic, revenge, and killings in every direction. It's best to mute your sorrow and hide your resentment, or share them with a companion in misfortune."

Francine Niyitegeka: "At the market, we sell to one another without a qualm. In the *cabaret*, we talk with them about farming, the weather, reconciliation; we share bottles and we exchange civil words of agreement . . . except about *that*.

"Hutus are not touched by the truth. They mention the killings in the *gaçaça* only through self-interest, to avoid prison and fines, when they are denounced by colleagues. If there were no reward, they wouldn't say a word about the killings. They talk through the force of the law and for the favor of the law. When they're drunk, they taunt one another or incriminate their comrades who are still in jail. One even hears former prisoners joking about how they'd do it again if the drought keeps up, because life is actually easier in prison than out in a sun-cracked field.

"But they never question a Tutsi, never ask, for example, how it was for us, what scars we still bear, whom did we lose, what was our life like then and what life is like for us now, without the strength and kindness of our dear departed . . . They're not curious at all, not a jot.

"If a Tutsi asks for some detail, the Hutu dodges the question. Even if it's to learn where the killer cut a relative, so as to go dig out the bones and cover them in Christian burial, the Tutsi gets nowhere.

"We, too, tend to want to forget a little. Embroidering memories, rehashing stories, comparing details—that can be bothersome, that can complicate an already burdensome day. But the Hutus—they evade absolutely everything. They only want to speak about the wonderful present. So we prefer to joke around. The more we talk, the more they tell us how nice they are, the more we let ourselves be softened up by niceness. That eases our anger. Not our distrust or suspicions, but the anger, yes."

Jean-Baptiste Munyankore: "We are not allowed to speak bluntly of the killings with the Hutus. During the *gaçaça*, we can ask anything, but otherwise it's forbidden. And during the *gaçaça*, we testify, we question, we accuse, they reply, and it's over. We do not quarrel. In casual talks, we cannot ask them for any disturbing details. We all toss polite remarks at one another that nobody ever remembers.

"In the *cabaret*, no one dares ask the others what it was really like unless he's gotten soused. Me, old as I am, I mustn't set a bad example. It's unthinkable for either side to provoke the other. If we dared, that would be useful, but we prefer to avoid squabbling; we feel a little pity, a little fear, some unease . . . We have been influenced by the authorities.

"For example, two people came to me at home to ask forgiveness. They did not come sincerely but to try to avoid prison. It's difficult to tell a father how you cut his daughter, or for the father to ask those people how they cut her. So we said nothing, just exchanged civilities. They offered a little drink; we promised to help one another with our farmwork. Listening to them, not listening to them, it was all the same. I listened so that they would go away sooner and leave me with my grief. As they left, those people topped off the visit by saying they had done me a kindness by failing to catch me in the marshes. I pretended to be grateful."

Sylvie Umubyeyi: "My feelings are changing. Ten years ago, if I tried talking about what I lived through during the genocide, I became too shaky, I couldn't go on. Whenever I ventured back into my story, emotions would boil up, my confidence would drain away, and panic would overpower me; I'd have to get out. It was too soon. Today, I've learned how to cope, thanks to a Belgian psychologist.

"I released my heart, not from fear but from helpless distress. If I'm telling my story, if I'm too upset by memories, I remain silent for a moment, thinking of the future, of the good things ahead of me, waiting for my emotions to subside. When my courage returns, I follow it back to my story.

"After the genocide, I'd lost confidence in everything. Well, my trust in other people . . . that obviously eroded, but my self-confidence—that has returned. Yes, I feel great hope for myself, and I can talk with others once again.

"I went in a professional capacity as a social worker to the prison in Butare, which confines many important figures of the genocide. We talked together about confessions, reconciliation, the effects of trauma. I was surprised: Those intellectuals are quite articulate. They draw strength from one another, write letters to the families of their victims, letters that are perhaps calculated, perhaps sincere. They are preparing for their release. They are poised, polite, seemingly willing to speak frankly—except about their wrongdoing, obviously.

"They don't in any way resemble the Hutus of the hills, who can be cowardly and ashamed, who must endure the sad faces of their neighbors and the bitter words of widows. Such Hutus are quick-tempered, they react too abruptly.

"I tell myself: This is not good. Those Hutu farmers are the majority, their arms are needed to feed the population. They know too many things they cannot reveal. If they give too much evidence, they'll harvest evil looks, threats from their neighbors—perhaps even from their own sons, who risk being accused as well. We must help them to speak, at least those who want to. It's an ancient obsession of Rwandan society, this suffering from one's own secrets.

"One day we received a small delegation of Hutus from northern Rwanda, up where the Hutus of the *akazu* live,[*] the stronghold of the Habyarimana family, pure Hutus who killed off their Tutsis so long ago they still think we have pointed ears. It was one of those obligatory reconciliation groups, here for little prayers and visits to the memorials.[†] We couldn't find a thing to say to one another beyond polite nothings.

[*] *In Kinyarwanda,* akazu *means household or family, and here it means the inner circle around the strongman in power. In 1993 it meant the clique of powerful northerners who organized the genocide, notably those around President Habyarimana's wife, Agathe Kanziga, and her three brothers.*

[†] *Many Tutsi men, assuming they would be the principal targets of Hutu violence, fled to the hills when the 1994 genocide began. But when women, children, and the elderly sought refuge in the churches, which had always provided sanctuary, they were horribly butchered there. The churches at Nyamata and Ntarama are now genocide memorial sites; at Nyamata, thousands of bones lie piled on shelves behind the nave; at Ntarama, the corpses have been left lying in situ, as they were at the moment of death. —Translator's note*

"We gathered for the farewell meal. We ate together in almost complete silence. The man sitting next to me said, 'I would never have believed that I would one day sit eating beside a Tutsi. Back home, no one will believe me.' We laughed, and he added, 'Personally, I was convinced that all Tutsis in the Bugesera thought only of killing us in revenge.' I told him, 'Well, I believed that all the Hutus in the north have been thinking of nothing but cutting Tutsis since 1959, the year when they got a really good start on the job.' We talked without any trouble. We were quite at ease because we were complete strangers: I had no idea what he'd done during the killings, and he didn't know anything about how I had survived.

"Soon afterward, that Hutu gentleman sent us a big busload of Hutus from the north in a second delegation. I thought, He knows as well as I do that our destinies will never find a chance to escape from Rwanda. We are going to live next to one another; we must talk together.

"As I told you the last time, neighbors have great importance in Rwandan custom. A neighbor is indeed the only person who knows how you woke up, what you need, whether you can help one another. If you no longer know your neighbor, or if that person slips away when you speak, you have lost such a great deal. Talking is a wind that blows neither forgiveness nor forgetting: that—impossible. But the soothing of peace, yes. Keeping quiet, though, stirs up misunderstandings, suspicions. It fans the flames of fear and hatred, and the temptation to snatch up the machete.

"If we do talk together, I am not sure they won't start up again. But if we remain silent, we're quite sure they are going to try. And if I, I who am a Tutsi, must take the first step because the Hutu in front of me feels too conflicted, I will start the dialogue—and tough luck if I end up the victim, because I could just as well win my wager. My heart can't always be on red alert."

. . .

Angélique Mukamanzi: "Myself, I no longer feel guilty for having survived. But to have a conversation with those Hutu people who saw everything, who rejoiced over the rags we wore, our misery, the mud we drank, the banana-plant sap we sucked thirstily—that would humiliate me. It would be anguishing. Telling them that we crawled in the fields to eat raw things with our bare hands, that some people even shared intimacies next to dead bodies—it would dishonor us.

"I have not yet told my boy Cédric the truth about the killings. He's only five. But it won't be a lesson of a single day. The child is already asking lots of questions. Why does his mama have no mama or papa? He doesn't understand why we don't get together with a family on Sundays. He might feel ashamed to hear that his grandpa was hacked up by machete in a slimy pool, and he might also be scared. It's hard to know what a little boy knows of this genocide that children are not supposed to talk about. He will find out everything, because he's already starting to learn things through the poison of hearsay."

Innocent Rwililiza: "We used to meet at Marie-Louise's place every evening to talk: a necessary ritual before going home. We'd remember, we'd wonder about things: how we'd suffered, how we'd escaped, the deaths, deprivations, disappointments. We'd go over and over it—and get a little tired of it. Later, some folks who hadn't lived through the killings started coming to the *cabaret*. We made friends with them, and didn't want to annoy them. Gradually we survivors went our separate ways as a matter of course.

"Today you'll find Tite at Chicago's, Dominique at the little *cabaret* across from the taxi-buses, yours truly at Kébissi. Of course, no one has forgotten. But we came to realize that those endless rehashings would keep us from fitting back into life properly. Many people don't want to talk about it anymore because they want to change their lives.

"As for the Kayumba Forest survivors, you can see Émmanuel is getting involved in district politics, Théoneste is undertaking some very profitable businesses along the new paved road, Eugénie is running her *cabaret*, while I'm a school principal. Some have become prosperous merchants, even deputies in Kigali, or plump and elegant wives.

"They don't want unpleasant rumors coming back about their rags and lice. They keep silent to escape what they fled from. The more you tell of your survival, the more you run yourself down in others' eyes. Many fear losing the esteem of their colleagues, because the survivor did everything possible to *survive*, not to live. Worse, those who were raped, who paid blood money, who were forced to go along and denounce their friends, as happened in Kigali or Butare, those who fled faster by shoving away a tiny child clutching their legs—they don't want to tell this to just anyone, especially not to foreigners or jeering Hutus. Or only if it's styled as a joke, to relieve their burden a little, to seem strong, or to make a pretense of neighborly friendliness.

"If a Tutsi talks to Hutu culprits about the killings, it's to learn details about the hunting expeditions, the victims' names, anything they said, the spots where they were cut, or buried, because the Tutsis saw almost nothing from where they were hiding. But otherwise, as for me, the why of our ordeal and how we survived—I refuse.

"Anyway, the survivors have no places where they can discuss this. At Mass they sing, pray, and it's over. In *cabarets* they banter together over a Primus about such matters, but you have to be careful: Hutus don't want to hear about all that foolishness, and they can get angry. The radio and television talk a lot about what happened. Many people explain the genocide, especially during the mourning period every April, but they avoid the truly devastating facts, names, cruel details, and speak of it as a lesson useful to both sides: to the Hutus, to tell them they must not do it again and should be docile and hardworking; to the Tutsis, to say they must accept reconciliation despite their misgivings, and be humble and make allowances, too.

"Basically it's the Tutsis from abroad, those of the former diaspora, who are running the show. These Tutsis suffered in exile and returned after the killings to reclaim houses, buy the most cows, start up new businesses. They bicker more easily over possessions than over killings. They are wary of the Hutus but do not fear them, and so they profit: they trade fine words with the Hutus, avoid quarrels, keep their sights on the future. They govern the country.

"And the survivors, they wind up frustrated, under a crippling inhibition, and they murmur . . . Being powerless to voice one's anger, sadness, and longing for what is lost, and unable to tell one's whole story for fear of offending a Hutu or annoying the authorities—this inability to reveal one's heart is sheer torture.

"I say this sincerely: survivors have no opportunity to express their true private feelings in public and to ask for a comforting little compensation.

"It's excruciating. For example, Claudine tells you in strict confidence that she hates the Hutus; Francine says she starts shaking when she looks into the face of a Hutu on the path; Berthe won't go to Mass anymore for fear of being seated next to a Hutu; Cassius can't speak to a Hutu girl; Marie-Louise no longer supervises her fields because the Hutu women nearby frighten her. The survivors are suffering from this restraint. If they were to open their hearts and spit out their feelings, it would bring them solace, but chaos for the country."

. . .

Berthe Mwanankabandi: "Between what we experienced and what they're saying now, the chasm keeps growing. They say it well, like a story prepared with horrible episodes of bloodletting. The content is there, all right; the facts are increasingly correct, and every detail seems to fit. But the emotional experience is disappearing because we can't speak of our feelings at the time. What's missing is what went on in the survivors' minds and hearts. The anguish endured can't be told, and it becomes less and less a reality.

"No one talks anymore about what was happening inside our heads. If you ask me about my thoughts, for example, I can only reply that perhaps I was thinking of many things: of God, or the death of God; of hiding myself and my charges; of my terror of the machete, or of loneliness; of no longer wanting to live. I saw myself being raped. Each evening I prepared myself to die the next day. But by thinking about what, really? I can produce a few sentences for your book, I can search for the right words to please you, yet I can't bring real precision to what I was thinking for so long, hiding out in the marshes or with my companions at night.

"Perhaps my thoughts flew away. Perhaps I stopped thinking, perhaps my thoughts about survival no longer resembled real thoughts. We were not completely ourselves anymore, and that is why we have forgotten. Because of this blackout with the survivors, there is a truth that will always elude anyone who did not live through the genocide."

A DIABOLICAL TRUTH

Off in the penitentiary, far from this cohabitation, Joseph-Désiré Bitero emphasizes not the difficulty of speaking but the danger of doing so. He does not mention the judicial risks, since the sterility of his trial testimony has already ensured his death sentence, or the vengeful threats of his victims' families, who he knows are powerless. He is thinking of a more existential danger.

Bitero was not born evil and did not grow up in an atmosphere of hatred. Quite the contrary: Like many great killers of history, at one period in his life he was cultured, friendly, a good father and good colleague. He was a nice kid, became a happy teacher, had no quarrel with his Tutsi neighbors. There is no sign of any traumatic event in his peaceful early existence in Gatare, a quiet neighborhood in Nyamata. When a cousin—the mayor—urged him to join the political party of President Habyarimana, Joseph-Désiré rose swiftly within the Party Youth Movement, then the *interahamwe*, and it was at the head of that militia that he spent three months planning and a good five weeks directing the killing expeditions in the district of Nyamata, hunts that murdered more than fifty thousand Tutsis out of a population of fifty-nine thousand.

I had last seen Joseph-Désiré Bitero four years earlier, in a garden on the grounds of the Rilima penitentiary, in the shade of an acacia whose branches drooped beneath the weight of splendid weaverbird nests. Nothing there has changed: neither the heat in the garden, nor the strident warbling of the birds, nor the man himself, who arrives with the same swing in his step, wearing his impeccably ironed pink uniform and some incongruous leather boxing shoes. The years on death row haven't touched his stocky physique. He still flashes his jolly smile and winks at everyone with the same old good-guy charisma. And that's exactly his problem: his understanding of the genocide seems to have frozen solid forever the day after the last machete blow. *Seems*, because it's impossible to figure out if this blindness is willing pretense, or a necessary ploy, or a mocking performance. He appears to take no critical distance. It simply never occurs to him that as the years go by, we on the outside might see him in a different light. He enjoys playing the role of an opposition figure, a combatant vanquished by his adversary, taking his defeat in stride—and with panache: "There are some situations that set you singing if you win or crying if you lose," he likes to say. A tireless orator, he has no sense of how empty his words are. To all appearances he feels nostalgic for the days when he taught school . . . and the time when he used to harangue his troops on the soccer field and believed in a better world, without Tutsis.

A shrewd politician, he claims he was a cog in a terrible machine, a scapegoat, and he rewrites history with that perverse profusion of detail so characteristic of revisionists, never suspecting how pathetic these efforts are, because although he still impresses his fellow inmates and retains a certain aura among those who are set free, he doesn't understand that sooner or later all these liberated killers will leave him, one by one, to his lucubrations. Impervious to the slightest remorse, he is also incapable of imagining how others see him.

Nevertheless, what he says about the danger of speaking today is interesting, because he emphasizes, unknowingly, the absolute nature of the genocide.

Joseph-Désiré Bitero: "Every civilized person must take responsibility for his or her actions. However, sometimes life presents you with actions you cannot claim out loud. Myself, I was the district leader of the *interahamwe* at the time of the killings. I did not comb the villages and the marshes, I did not wield the machete more than others did, but I accepted that responsibility. Accepting such a truth is not something just anyone can do. Admitting to so grave a sin—that requires more than simple courage. And speaking about the details of something so extraordinary, well, it can be hellish: for the person speaking as well as for the one who listens. Because afterward, society can hate you beyond all understanding if you reveal a situation that society does not wish to believe: a truth it calls inconceivable.

"We here on death row, we talk above all about the Congo years, because that was a harrowing time. We also discuss our case files. We deal with the killings if the occasion arises—for example, if we read an article or hear a radio program, and we speak truths about the genocide that no one else says aloud.

"For example, I say this: it's the Patriotic Front, after all, that massacred a great many Hutus in the camps in Congo. A great many babies and old mamas died for nothing in Kivu. Personally, I can say that I'm a revisionist because I'm a former *interahamwe* leader and a prison inmate. But who can say that in Rwanda, except from inside a penitentiary or outside our borders, like that French judge Bruguière* or those French writers? They're a good thing, the revisionists' books. My colleagues and I discuss them a

* *See page 241.*

lot, because it's our whole truth that's coming out on those pages. On death row, we enjoy reading and rereading those books. We encourage the authors and their friends. They clearly explain that the Hutu camp premeditated the genocide of the Tutsis only to defend ourselves against the attacks of the *inkotanyi*, and that the genocide was both definitely planned and definitely avoidable.

"We'd been too afraid, it's true. We believed that the *inkotanyi*, once installed on the throne, would be especially oppressive— that the Hutus would be pushed back into their fields and robbed of their words. We told ourselves we didn't want to be demeaned anymore, made to wash the Tutsi ministers' air-conditioned cars, for example, the way we used to carry the kings in hammocks. I was raised in fear of the return of Tutsi privileges, of obeisance and unpaid forced labor, and then that fear began its bloodthirsty march. I came to manhood at the worst moment in Rwandan history, educated in absolute obedience, in ethnic ferocity. My colleagues and I sift through a lot of that in good comradeship. We might squabble or take a swipe at one another over a mess tin of porridge or a lousy sleeping spot, but never over ideas.

"Humans are human, even on death row. If a man has a chance to keep quiet about a dreadful, perhaps diabolical truth, he will try to silence it forever. Too bad if his silence makes him seem like a throwback to native savagery."

WHO CAN TAKE A PICTURE
OF FEAR?

The movie people are here! There had been rumors about this for months, and they've actually been spotted this morning in Nyamwiza, at the edge of the marshes.

When we arrive atop the butte overlooking a slow loop of the river, about thirty vans are parked near a village of tents. Technicians are bustling around and generators are rumbling. This is nothing like the innumerable film crews who have already crisscrossed the region: now an American super-production is here to film *Sometimes in April*, a saga directed by a famous Haitian filmmaker with a screenplay that took three years to write and required several months of scouting all over the country. The baptism of cinema is a spectacular event in a place where people don't even know what a real movie theater looks like.

A hundred meters below, a second camp on the steep slope protects the crew members from the heat. Kitted out in bush shirts, chic overalls, and rubber boots, they're all clutching walkie-talkies and bottles of mineral water.

Down at the water's edge, here's the scene: a camera mounted on tracks; fake corpses lying in the muck; a loudspeaker blaring directions; a naked, mud-splattered boy who pops in and out of the papyrus for take after take. Suddenly, a scream; later, another one. According to a French daily reporting on the shoot, some Rwandan survivors are cracking under the strain of their intense emotions. Actually, the problem is that some of the women technicians can't bear visualizing sequences that are too violent, and then they are immediately engulfed by a "pool" of production psychologists. Later, an angry murmur spreads through the crowd. The French daily will claim that local farmers cannot repress their fright or rage at the sight of the machetes, when in reality they've just learned that the twenty-dollar wage for which they showed up at five a.m.—a godsend during this dry season—will be paid only to those who are hired as extras.

Aside from this incident, in spite of the heat, the hundreds of onlookers crouching on the grass remain eerily silent, stunned by an enterprise that is to them unthinkable: to make a muddy kid rehearse and play this scene of killing. And they will talk about *that* for days.

Sitting beside Innocent Rwililiza during a discussion about images, I describe to him the retrospective amazement of several friends, cameramen and photographers who traveled through Nyamata at the time of the killings, taking pictures of the destruction and desolation there without suspecting that only fifteen kilometers away in the marshes there were manhunts going on. We wind up talking about the lack of photographs or filmed images of the genocide, a problem that soundly trips up every director who shoots a film on the subject. I tell Innocent that during the Second World War, a conflict that was filmed and photographed in every possible way from Stalingrad to El Alamein and from Pearl Harbor to Dresden, the Shoah—that war within the war—left astonishingly few images of arrests and deportations, still less of the machinery of death itself in the eastern European countryside or in the camps. Innocent thinks that's a lucky thing.

Intrigued, in the days that follow I speak about this with several Rwandan survivors, who surprise me by agreeing with Innocent. Their explanations, like those of Innocent Rwililiza and Berthe Mwanankabandi, prove limpidly clear.

Innocent: "Survivors are no longer masters of their memories and cannot rid themselves of painful recollections. Setting them aside, filing them elsewhere, that is possible with shameful memories of lice, a rape, or a small betrayal, for example. But erasing them—impossible. Any survivor who tries that will see them return with increased malignancy and must therefore try to live with all those disturbing mental images that have taken on a stubborn life of their own. Fortunately, survivors can keep certain images to themselves, without showing the ugliest and most hideous ones to someone who wasn't there. Even though survivors know their companions may have identical images in their own memories, such pictures are not exchanged like words. And with the passage of time, after all, survivors are reassured: they feel safer, review those images less often, feel less and less disturbed.

"During the yearly mourning period in April, many pictures of the genocide—photos of skeletons and corpses in particular—are made public on television and in newspapers or exhibits. I can accept that, because they are pictures from after the genocide. One almost never sees pictures taken during the killings, and it doesn't surprise me that there are almost no images of killings during the other genocides—of the Jews or Armenians. There aren't any photos because there is no place for photographers on killing fields, such as our marshes and forests. No pathway of any kind along which a foreigner might slip among the killers, the

killed, and those who have yet to be killed. No place for an out-
sider, who would never, ever survive.

"This is most fortunate, because images of the killings under
way—I could not bear that. Can you imagine a snapshot of
Eugénie running through the forest with her *pagne* up around her
waist, or Marie-Louise hiding in the doghouse with the dog and
all its shit? It would be degrading. And a photo of little gatherings
of supplicants beneath the papyrus, of hacked-up people crawling
to moisten their lips in marsh water, or even famished old folks
clawing the dirt for scraps of manioc? Pictures of our monkey life
in Kayumba or their reptile life in the marshes would be inhuman. It would pile pain on the sufferings of the survivors and be
useless besides. Because those pictures would make nothing more
explicit to people who did not experience the genocide, and
would simply illustrate a dance of death."

Berthe: "While we hid beneath the papyrus, we wondered
silently, Is it today that I will die, is it tomorrow, will I suffer
awfully from the machete blade before the end? Will the agony
last long? The same impressions, over and over: the waiting, the
fear, and more fear. Who can photograph those kinds of feelings
in the marshes? Who can take a picture of a mama clutching her
infant beneath her *pagne* as she listens to a small band of *interahamwe* wade past her in the water? The fugitives could exchange
looks, quite probably of encouragement or fright. Some fugitives
seemed so panicked and disheartened that you could see it in
their eyes. Who can take a picture of those looks, and the ones
we gave to the scattered clumps of bodies when we came out of
the mire at sundown? Could we have accepted the company of a
photographer in the marshes as if at a wedding, knowing that we
were all waiting to be butchered?"

.   .   .

Innocent: "A genocide must be photographed before the killings—to show clearly the preparation, the faces of the leaders, the stockpiled machetes, the complicity of the French soldiers or the Belgian priests, the careful organization of the hunting expeditions. In my opinion, pictures of the preambles and the premeditation are the only important ones for allowing foreigners to understand the mechanics of the thing.

"And the genocide can be photographed afterward—to show the corpses, the survivors' haggard faces, the arrogance or shame of the killers, the churches piled high with bones, the events in Congo and Canada, the penitentiaries, the ceremonious foreigners visiting the memorials. To convince disbelieving minds and thwart negationists.

"But the intimate truth of the genocide belongs to those who lived it, and so does the right to withhold this truth, for it is not something to be shared with just anyone."

WITH DEATH AND THE DEAD

Marie-Louise Kagoyire: "I was offered up to death, which missed me, but I felt it stalking me and brushing past. Since then it has grown less fearsome, less grasping, more natural. Before, when death caught someone on the hill, it was a shocking moment. After all those dead bodies during the killings, though, it doesn't affect us the same way today. If a dear friend dies, I feel devastated. If it's the last oldster in a family line, I am saddened. But frightened, no. At the burial, we no longer share the anguish of before."

Berthe Mwanankabandi: "There was no pity for the dead in the marshes. Nobody thought about burying them, there were too many of them, we couldn't possibly. The sight of their nudity touched us in a horrifying way: those bodies hardly reminded us at all anymore of living people. We didn't bother with ceremonies for the unlucky ones who'd been cut; we simply said they'd been unlucky. Death was an everyday thing, from morning till night, so we no longer paid attention to the fate of corpses. Naturally, we might happen to spread a bit of mud over one of them, an acquaintance or a relative, but as to the others, we were too overwhelmed to deal with them.

"Of course, before I confronted the genocide, I was too

scared of death to look it in the face. It seemed rare, extraordinary. Two or three years might pass on the hill before death came to fetch someone we would accompany with tears to the grave.

"By the end of the killings, after encountering so many naked, decaying bodies, after stepping over them, finding them in the water of my hiding places, death became nothing to me. I mean, I had almost stopped paying any attention to the mystery of death. The news of a neighbor's passing did not affect me much.

"That lasted for years after the genocide. We buried casually, without digging deep, without gathering flowers, without putting on a pretty dress. We felt freed from death. Then the foreigners came to help us. Humanitarian workers taught us to reconsider the remains of our families murdered in the swamps, to try gathering them, imagining them as normal bodies. They drew us into funeral processions; they taught us modern attitudes of humanity, and reinstated elaborate ceremonies. They pushed us, as if they feared we would never again give a spit about the terrifying power of death.

"Sometimes sleep takes me back into the marshes. I see again all those people stretched out in the slime and soaking in blood. In a dream I see my parents, my little sisters, friends. I see living people who look like those dead bodies. Things seem normal, it's calm. It's good. I am with them and they sleep quietly, as if they had died. When I awake, I feel an awful anguish, or heavy grief, as if I had gone to the land of the dead."

Angélique Mukamanzi: "I was hunted like a game animal, but I have become a person again. My human nature pulls me forward. Reason why my memory sometimes fools me. It sets aside my bad thoughts to grant me some relief; it sorts through the memories and rejects sorrows that are too heavy. It doesn't want to linger always on that existence in the marshes, and that's only natural.

"So if I tell you about it, something will be missing. What it was like to exist as human prey is something that only those who died as prey could dare remember faithfully and recount truthfully."

Francine Niyitegeka: "Death isn't an anguish anymore. I'm not waiting expectantly for it, but it no longer scares me. Death brings rest, as well. In the marshes, we could see that the dead were now beyond all threats, pursuits, and especially machete blades. We saw peaceful corpses, we could envy their rest, but still we hid because we couldn't stop trying to escape our deathblows. Our fear of the machetes and of suffering was worse than our fear of death. Going back to hide in the marshes in the morning, we jumped over bodies with no thought of burying them. Leaving in the evening, we were too discouraged to have any thoughts at all.

"Now many people want to make up for lost time. Ceremonies seem to be more substantial than they were before the genocide. One can notice little changes. Some folks tend to spruce up the rituals, especially if they've seen funerals in the films on television or traveled to Europe, where they handle tombs and processions better.

"Me, I don't pay attention anymore to the uneasy atmosphere at funerals. If they drag on too long, I might well joke about it or sigh with a friend. But if it's to bury some bones from 1994—found in a ditch, for example, and being placed in the memorial—then I feel my heart quiver.

"The killers trapped me beneath the papyrus. They tore my child from my arms. They macheted him and just dropped him into the swamp. I was clubbed on the head. When I came to, I found neither tears to cry nor words to comfort myself. I no

longer had enough intelligence for sadness. My little one had
been cut. My head hurt. In the marshes, deep inside ourselves,
we had no questions left. Except: Will there be a big hunt the
next day? Will I be hacked up like the others? Questions about
immediate torments, so to speak. Understanding what was going
on, constructing philosophies, reflecting on the shame or despair
of a mama losing her child to the killers' machetes, that never
happened.

"The death and fear inside us listened to the silence and kept
us from wondering about things. The bodies in the marshes were
beyond our natural understanding."

Berthe Mwanankabandi, a few months later: "Living in the
marshes without any of the decent, ordinary thoughts about life
and death, having to step over decomposing corpses each morning and all the new ones of that day every evening—this feeds
memories that stretch into infinity. Those bodies abandoned
naked to time . . . the mutilated bodies of old mamas, young
girls, everybody—they were a bad dream come true.

"Yes, we can talk about the dead, we can bear witness to their
plight, we can supply details about the hunts and our mad flights
and the shouting and the fear. But we cannot talk about death
because we escaped that.

"Survivors are missing something they need to describe the
genocide. Everything we saw and heard—we can report that:
blows, falls, whisperings in the last moments, sprawled corpses.

"And yet, for death, we cannot bear witness except by looking sideways. I can say: I saw this person moldering away naked
in the bog; I heard killers laughing and the screams of the poor
woman; I even heard the sound of the blade on her muscles. But
the wretched woman's feelings before the machete, her look into
the eyes of the killer, her mute words when she falls cut to the

bone, her innermost thoughts if she is stripped or raped . . . about that, I myself ought to say nothing. The dead have gone away with their secrets, which the corpses may only hint at.

"Telling the story doesn't bring them back to life, since we cannot overcome their death. Telling only offers them some kindness and dignity. It's reaching out to their memory the best way we can. Showing, whenever we get the chance, that they were worthy people.

"Reason why, to me, it's a serious problem to recount those deadly hunts only when we're encouraged to do so, on days of remembrance when the dead become a nameless mass, for example during the mourning period in April, or the *gaçaça* trials beneath the tree, or when a foreigner like you passes by.

"Casual encounters never lead to honest stories about the dead—with the sincerity of intimacy, is what I mean. And yet these well-known and dearly beloved dead are the most necessary people to remember when telling about the genocide."

Sylvie Umubyeyi: "Obviously, I view death differently today. It doesn't normally frighten me anymore. Before the killings, I was too scared of death even to dare go near a coffin. Now, if I hear someone has died, I go to the hospital or the cemetery, and think: Well, the time had come, it's over now, this person was very ill and now is gone. Death is no longer a touchy matter, a metaphysical thing for me. When I hear the funeral service, see the nice clothes in the procession, listen to the words of praise for the deceased, I don't feel any emotion now. I wait patiently. We saw corpses being stripped, dogs eating bodies, girls rotting spitted on sticks shoved between their legs, lying around the countryside like trees and everything else. The genocide killed off the sanctity of death in Rwanda.

"I no longer fear my own death. The way I feel, that's where

I was supposed to go, that's where I will go. I mean it. Except if I must be cut down by machetes. Yes, I'm terrified of machetes. If I encounter a farmer with his blade on his shoulder, I panic. But going? No. I'm waiting."

Innocent Rwililiza: "It was not important that we couldn't bury the dead. We weren't sorry about it, we couldn't stop for it, we had to keep going. We, too, were candidates for death and knew perfectly well we'd end up like them. We truly understood that we could do nothing human for them and no one could do any better for us, when our turn would soon arrive. We realized that even our deaths would be as worthless as those last days we were living. We had no trouble eating beside cadavers, sleeping in the same bushes with them.

"At the time, we felt twinges of distress over not taking care of the dead as usual, but that was only normal. At first it did bother me, but not much, because I didn't know many of the dying, or not very well. Today I feel no remorse at all. If I had come across the bodies of my wife or parents, perhaps I would think differently. Sometimes, when I go to the memorial with a visitor, I look at the skulls lined up on the shelves and catch myself studying little details, like the teeth, as if I were hoping in spite of myself to recognize those of my wife or my son, who were cut down in the church.

"What Berthe says is true: there are facts and feelings we can manage to describe, and others, no; only the dead could report them if they were here, and we must not describe these things in their name. Why? Because they alone here fully experienced the genocide, so to say. It's not possible to speak in place of the departed, because everyone has a personal way of telling that story. Marie-Louise has her own way, Berthe hers, Jean-Baptiste his. The dead have theirs, which would be even more different, since they would be telling their story while holding death by the hand.

"A dead person, for example, having begged for mercy and seen this plea scorned by the killer, or having watched the fatal blow to the neck descend and felt the spurt, or having sighed out one last breath, all naked in the mud, or having blurted out certain words for the first—and last—time in this life, such a person would describe death right to the end and reach a full stop.

"Still, in general, survivors can talk about the genocide in collaboration with the dead, after all, by being explicit about precisely that point. Because the dead exist in our narratives. They are dead to the living, but they have never disappeared for the survivors: I mean that a certain complicity keeps them closer to survivors than to other living souls. They listen to us; they bring us happiness or sorrow. If I reminisce about my first wife, Rose, and our child, they provide the dignity that is missing from what I can say."

Jean-Baptiste Munyankore: "By the end, I had lost all my dear ones in the marshes. I was left alone with two neighbors with whom I'd been fleeing the hunters: another old teacher like me, and his wife. We three always hid together, sharing whispers and looks in our hiding place. In the evenings their children would help us by bringing food they'd scrounged in abandoned fields. In exchange, we would offer the advice of long experience.

"One day the wife was slaughtered an arm's length from my secret spot. I heard the screams offering money, the cries for mercy, the blows. I said nothing, I did not raise my eyes; I saw nothing. Only after the killers had left did I look out at the naked woman in the blood and mire.

"Now there were two, the gentleman and I. We became inseparable, hiding by day and sleeping on the hill at night. While

I was an optimist, he was a pessimist: opposites, we formed a team. We slept side by side. We'd talk then, but never face to face: one would look off to the right, the other to the left, as if to watch for danger on all sides and to avoid each other. We'd discuss the people cut down that day, how they died. We'd wonder if the *inkotanyi* were advancing; we'd whisper encouragements.

"Every night we'd say farewell, in case we didn't meet again the next evening. We looked at each other only when we heard the first gunshots of the killers in the distance, so we could hare off to the marshes together. In our hiding place we'd stare down at the water in front of us, because we knew that our shining eyes might draw those of a killer, and also we didn't want to dishearten each other by sharing frightened glances. We looked at each other only when we crept out of the papyrus. We were gradually becoming the same person. After the disappearance of his younger brother, who had been considered for a position as a government minister in Kigali, the gentleman lost strength more rapidly. One day, out in the papyrus, he just stood up and began to jump and run despite the *interahamwe*. He was cut down in his flight; still in the hiding place, I didn't budge. I was left alone, but I kept whispering to myself the same things that we had once whispered to each other.

"There was nothing we could do for the dead. When the killings of the day hadn't been too bad, though, and we felt relieved as we went back up the hill, we might lay a few bodies out carefully at the edge of the marsh and cover them kindly with leaves. We didn't do that often.

"In the evening, when people were still in their death agonies, we managed to pray with them so that they would be properly welcomed in heaven. We might try to exchange farewells. I can mention my nephew and my sister and others whose names

I have forgotten. For example, my sister told me, 'After I'm gone, take my children, they're yours.'

"The dying were divided into two categories, depending on their temperaments. There were those who screamed at death, who howled at the *interahamwe*. Some of them even almost fell over dead before being butchered, and were so distraught with fear that they would suddenly cry out, anticipating the first strike of the machete, thereby attracting the killers' attention."

"And yet some people died calmly, offering encouragement. They'd say, 'Goodbye, hide carefully, it's all over for me, but you—keep trying to hold out till the very end.' Some brave old people expired quietly, saying that they would finally find rest, that they wanted to leave us a bit of comfort. There were even some who turned to suicide. We told them to hang on until the fatal day, but they didn't want to wait any longer.

"I remember two oldsters, deaf to our pleas, who were losing their courage. They had observed that many young people had been killed and that soon there wouldn't be enough of them left to bring food back to the others in the evening. They saw themselves left helpless, defeated before the final blow, and they dreaded ending up as beggars. They didn't want to expose themselves to the killers' mockery and insults or beg to be killed cleanly with a single blow. They were tired of the humiliation: that's what they explained to us. They swallowed a can of concentrated insecticide and left us, moaning. Another old fellow, one morning, refused to go hide in the marshes. 'I'm not slinking around in the muck anymore,' he said. 'I'm staying right here.' He sat down on his chair calmly, to look at his field the way he always had before. That evening we found he'd been cut down almost without moving from his seat.

"One day there was a horrific hunt. April 30. In the evening the killers left so many dead and dying in the swamps that the survivors who crawled out of the mud half believed they were corpses themselves. We heard death agonies in every direction. Even as we slogged through the swamp, we no longer felt truly alive.

"I have no regrets for not burying the dead properly. Death had lost its mystery. We ran, we hid, we rested, we tried to hold on, we had no respect for anything anymore, least of all death. There was no more decent sadness or dignity left. Seeing death in such vast numbers, a stinking, everyday thing, made what we'd learned in catechism class unbelievable.

"These days, death has perked up again. When someone dies, I'm saddened, I put on a suit, and I cry with everyone else."

Eugénie Kayierere: "A person cut down right in front of me, I never saw that, because we were racing too quickly to linger and look. It happened behind us. I heard, I sensed the blows, but I never watched.

"However, some people who had just been hacked up were still alive and implored us as we went by, showing their arms and legs cut short by the machete, calling to us, but no one dared stop because we simply had to run. Sometimes we jumped over the dying. They wanted to be finished off, wanted us to bring them something to drink, wanted medicinal herbs for their pain. It was impossible.

"Evenings, when we gathered together, if they were unlucky enough to still be alive, some of these wounded would murmur, 'Finish me, help me end my suffering.' We would cover the dying with branches, but deliver the fatal blow? No one could do it. We could let them savor water in their mouths and words of comfort in their ears, and that was really it.

"We were pursued, we ran all day, we waited through sleepless nights, and we have soldiered on for years since then, yes. But our ordeal stops at the gates of death. What is behind those gates belongs to the dead.

"Describing the way the dead were demeaned, chopped up so viciously, is dishonorable to them. Giving details about how they were stripped naked or cut short, how they dragged themselves along, how they pleaded for mercy, how they screamed or groaned or vomited or bled—that can be humiliating for them. One must be polite even to the dead, respecting their privacy. Talking about one's own experience is all right. But one shouldn't speak of what others have been through, especially the dead."

Élie Mizinge: "In the Nyamwiza marshes, the papyrus smelled more of death than of slime. That's the only thing that bothered us, but not enough to frighten us off dealing out more death. It was the odor we resented, not death. Actually, death made a coward of me only in the penitentiary.

"We, the killers, we've forgotten none of our fateful misdeeds. The lives we took are well lined up in our memories. Those who claim the contrary prove themselves liars. In prison I remembered the dead in the swamps, and I thought, Since you cut so many people, you will be killed in your turn. Whenever I thought of the marsh corpses, I shook worse from fear than from a fit of malaria. Later, when I was pardoned, the fear went away. I felt cured of all that."

Ignace Rukiramacumu: "The corpses were rotting so fast. We couldn't recognize the ones we'd caught. We saw death at almost every step, and yet we never envisioned our own or that of our families. Death became both ordinary and unnatural; what I mean is, we stopped paying attention to it . . . During the genocide, not for a single day did I think death could whip round to claim me brutally in turn. The truth of the genocide is in the mouths of both the killers, who manipulate and conceal it, and the dead, who have carried it away with them."

Alphonse Hitiyaremye: "Having killed a lot and seen so much killing hasn't made me more wary of death; if it scares me more now, it's only because in Congo, I was convinced I was going to die. During the killings, we never thought about the fear of death. And that's what really seems extraordinary to me.

"The survivors always feel death at their heels. They meet an evil look, hear a shout—and they jump sideways. Their uneasiness unnerves us, too. As for a killer, if he goes back to his land, he doesn't feel pursued by anything, not even the stench of death he worked in every day."

THE NOISY SERENADE OF
LITTLE BIRDS

Unable to cultivate his fields for several years, Innocent Rwililiza finally resigned himself to entrusting his land, which lies on the eastern slope of Kibungo Hill, to Marthe Mukashumba, a Hutu lady deserted by her husband. Overjoyed at this windfall, Marthe fixed up the old cobwall house, moved her six children in, and set resolutely to work clearing brush, tilling, sowing.

Today, the five acres form two fields separated by the road, the uphill one planted with beans, the one below boasting a promising young banana plantation that extends down to a small wood marking the lower boundary of the property. Innocent and Marthe, pleased with their cooperation, are planning a coffee-tree plantation like the ones that flourished in the region before the genocide.

One afternoon I am chatting in that new banana plantation with Father Boniface, a shy priest from Kibungo. We are out of earshot of his gossipy flock, but then a swarm of kids turns up out of nowhere. The smallest, three or four years old, are carrying two-liter jerry cans, while the big kids lug twenty-liter models almost as heavy as they are. It's the after-school hour for fetching water and, having spotted our small truck parked beside the field, they have invaded the plantation. To shoo them off, we promise to drive them and their water back up the hill later on, if they will let us continue our conversation in peace.

Two hours later we return to the road, and to my amazement the children are all in a circle around the vehicle, a little worried about my intentions, sitting silent and still, jerry cans set down between their legs. A white person is a *muzungu*, a "usurper," and they've never been so close to one before. All the kids are barefoot; many wear simply some pants, a sweater, or a ragged bit of *pagne*, and a few girls are in their school uniforms. At the signal, they scramble into the back of our truck, helping one another hoist up the jerry cans.

We've hardly gotten going when I hear a din unlike any I've ever heard before, a kind of chorus or symphony of laughter. Through the back window I can see the kids standing or crouching, holding on to the sides as best they can, exhilarated, radiant, cackling, giggling, crowing, grinning ear to ear and laughing fit to bust. They have never been in any motor vehicle—many of them won't have another crack at one for years, since nobody in Kibungo owns one—and here they are going for a ride! They're ecstatic. They adore the bumps, the wind rushing by, the roar of the motor, and they warble songs, French nursery rhymes from school, hymns: they sing out everything they know.

Of course we abandon the track climbing directly to the village and take another one that circles up the hill, a jolting roller-coaster ride that disappears into groves of trees whose branches tickle the passengers, swings around a massive tree trunk, breaks up into ruts, and crosses paths with herds of livestock. Behind the cab, they're singing their heads off, rejoicing and waving extravagantly—triumphantly—to everyone coming home from the fields.

At nightfall, up at the village, the kids scatter toward their houses, dragging along their jerry cans. When the children sneak a last look back at the van, the happiness gleaming in their eyes lights up the twilight.

Set on the flat summit of the hill, the center of Kibungo village lies along the track that climbs steeply from the river and then descends both to the right—in a gentle slope toward Nyarunazi and Ntarama, down to the newly paved main road to Nyamata— and to the left, toward the marshes, to the houses of Pio and Fulgence and, much farther along, to Alphonse's home in his tropical jungle.

Almost no one lives in central Kibungo anymore; most of the former inhabitants were Tutsis who chose to move to a *mudugudu*, where they feel safer among themselves, living close together, leaving their former, now rather dilapidated houses to be used as barns or storage sheds. And the Hutus prefer to stay on their farms, where they have always lived, near their fields and at a distance from their neighbors, at least until they, too, will be obliged to move to a *mudugudu*.

So Kibungo awakens at the first touch of sunshine in a mostly animal atmosphere: there's no barking, for in Africa dogs are not used for work and get very little to eat; but goats bleat, cows moo impatiently in their pens or, more contentedly, on their way together through the town to their grazing out in the bush, and of course the local birds make a hubbub (long-tailed souimangas, hummingbirds, and the parrotlike crested green turacos) along with their migrating brethren (weaverbirds, storks, and swallows). These myriads of birds, relieved or anxious at the dawning light, now seem—in their trees, thickets, and hideaways under the eaves—like the real denizens of Kibungo.

Aside from the drunks who have collapsed during the night

beneath a handy awning, and the discreet herdsmen, always dressed in rags both to disguise their employers' wealth and because their clothes are always being torn by branches, the first people abroad at daybreak are women. After placing their babies in shady spots, nestled in rolled-up *pagnes*, they let out the poultry and set up their sewing machines. They spread cloths on the ground where they will later shell beans by flailing them with long rods. They prop sacks of manioc against the wall of the mill-house, to be turned into the day's flour, and go light the fire in their back courtyards.

After checking their fields, some men arrive on bikes or pushing wooden wheelbarrows. They transport stems of bananas for the fermentation of *urwagwa*, start up an oil-fired generator, get the carpenters' and mechanics' workshops going. And they study the sky, worrying about the weather like everyone else in the world, except that here their anxieties are now compounded by the metaphysical dread of punishment.

At eight o'clock, floods of schoolchildren appear from every direction, as girls in blue and boys in khaki stream from the village toward the three brick structures of the former colonial triangle—the school, the church, and the government office building—set around a stony patch of ground where boys play soccer all day. The sturdier fellows monopolize the school's leather ball, which bounces around at the whim of successive waves of players from sunup to sundown, while the little kids use balls of banana leaves tied up with string. Some pint-size virtuosos perform maneuvers that would leave our recruiting scouts bug-eyed.

As for the adults, they shun the real playing field a little way down the track, in spite of its grass and regulation goalposts, because that's where the killers of the hunting expeditions gathered every morning in the spring of 1994. Pio, for example, loves soccer and never stopped playing it in the penitentiary, except when an epidemic was raging. He comes down to Nyamata on Sundays sometimes to watch the matches on TV between two Kigali teams, but he doesn't play here in town anymore. He doesn't dare. And he won't admit it, claiming instead that he has too much work to do on his new house.

Claudine's husband, Jean-Damascène, a survivor of the marshes, no longer puts on his soccer cleats either, not since his transfer to the primary school in Kibungo, even though professional clubs from the capital once eyed him covetously when he played as a sweeper for Bugesera Sport, a Nyamata team. He now contents himself with refereeing the kids' games. On Sundays, thanks to young players drawn from afar by bonuses under the sponsorship of a few enterprising leading citizens—a local contractor, Eugène Higiro; Dédé-Léonard, the medical orderly; and Muligo, director of the penitentiary—the Bugesera Sport team is once again delighting the crowds at the playing field in Nyamata.

But in Kibungo, no one feels like playing together anymore.

In the afternoon people gradually drift "downtown" and Kibungo comes alive: they've walked up from the fields, had a bite and freshened up at home, and have come here to see the day out. Cheerful and sweet, Fifi now opens her *cabaret* and stocks up on *urwagwa, ikigage,* Primus, Mutzig, and sometimes even *kanyanga,* an illegal rotgut distilled from *urwagwa.*

Always elegant, Francine opens her *cabaret* on weekends. There she especially welcomes the stock-breeding friends of her husband, Théoneste, who's been putting on weight ever since he lost his seat as a municipal councilor (for lack of a diploma) and began devoting himself entirely to his cattle. Those who buy a Primus go inside to savor it; those gathering to drink *urwagwa* sit on the benches outside, while others saunter around, on the lookout for the friendly offer of a bottle.

Indifferent to the wear and tear of his sixty-five years of farm labor, Ignace covers the five kilometers of bush between his house and the village every single day, because he can no longer bear to stay home as he used to. And yet he lives in an enchanting spot, at the end of a path buried in wild vegetation.

Constructed with durable materials and roofed with Belgian tiles laid over a ceiling of reeds, his large house is typical of Hutu dwellings in the Gitarama region. This one still hints at its former opulence, in spite of cracks in the walls and other stigmata from the time of its owner's imprisonment. Built on a ridge of Nganwa, a hill overlooking the Akanyaru River, and shaded from behind by an imposing *umunzenze* tree, the house sits above a steep slope that offers one of the most magnificent panoramas in the entire area.

Below a field cleared with maniacal care and tended from dawn to dusk by Ignace's wife with the occasional help of a day laborer or two, yellow-flowering trees cover the tortuous gullies of a dramatically red hillside. Farther down, the bright green of a banana plantation and celadon swaths of palm trees are outlined by the black bands left behind by peat fires. Beyond lies the fascinating vastness of the marshes that cover the invisible waters of the Akanyaru River, which one can somehow sense is almost motionless. The marshes stretch like a sea of foliage all the way to a hazy horizon of mountainous foothills.

The morning sun's slanting rays spark dazzling reflections from this palette of greens, which will later flatten out beneath the diaphanous afternoon light. In the evening, when the sun tips behind those foothills, it gilds the marshes with an orangey yellow before bathing them in a strange pink glow. On rainy days the gray sky and almost coal-black darkness of the clouds above the mountains transform yet again this realm of papyrus, water lilies, reeds, and the stocky aquatic trees called *kimbazi*.

When Ignace claims that his advanced age exempted him from leaving on the killing expeditions every morning from up in Kibungo, his argument in his own defense is understandable: he and a few former neighbors could go directly to work from their own homes and poach Tutsis without any useless detours.

In his yard, we listen to a concert of hummingbirds, plus the shouts of his daughters from the house next door whenever they're tormenting his new wife. On the path down to the water, however, new birdsongs ring out, the clamor of flamingos or the laughter of crested green turacos, answered by the whistling of *talapoin* monkeys, the grunting of wild pigs, and assorted mysterious cries.

You can lose yourself in admiration of the landscape. Sometimes you wonder yet again how it could ever have been the backdrop to one of the most ferocious massacres of the twentieth century, and you think of the bucolic images of forests that have erased all traces of a concentration camp, images created by Claude Lanzmann in his Holocaust documentary film *Sobibor*. Sometimes you also wonder, for the umpteenth time, how those killings in Rwanda could have gone on for so many long weeks in such an exposed landscape—within sight of all the hills and surrounding mountains, or visible from the sky by plane or helicopter—without any French, Burundian, or UN soldiers lobbing over a shell to interrupt them.

And then those endlessly looping questions without answers come to mind: questions about the Holocaust. Why, in a Germany blanketed with Allied air force bombs that reduced cities and industrial zones to rubble, did not a single bomb fall on one of those railway lines so clearly visible on the plains of Germany's and Poland's potato fields, railways that carried deportation trains from all over Europe toward the six extermination camps? Why did none of the eighty-five convoys deporting French Jews to the camps run into any obstacles, any sabotage by the French Resistance, which derailed or blocked dozens of other trains transporting munitions, supplies, troops, and sometimes political prisoners? Why did no partisan operation attack a train either in a station or out in the countryside, an act that would have delivered—along with the Jews crammed in the cattle cars—a vital message about the extermination already under way?

Of all the guys in the gang, Ignace seems the most impenetrable. It's impossible to read the thoughts behind his weathered face, with its eternal joking or sarcastic smile. He's cunning, often cynical, but sometimes astonishingly sincere as well when talking about himself and the killings. For example, he told me this in Rilima four years ago: "It is just as damaging to tell the truth to the justice system, to the population, or to yourself. Even in your heart of hearts, it is riskier to remember than to forget. Reason why I try to keep quiet with myself. The time to hear the truth about these things surpassing ordinary crimes will wait."

Innocent Rwililiza, who had sat with me as a trusted aide and interpreter when I interviewed the killers at Rilima, considers Ignace the worst—the *foulest*—of the gang. Innocent is even more repelled by Ignace than by Joseph-Désiré Bitero, who was his friend and colleague until three months before the first expeditions but who, as an *interahamwe* official, led killers into the very church where Innocent's wife and son were massacred. Probably because of his own childhood memories, Innocent sees Ignace as a personification of the Hutus' visceral, ancestral hatred of Tutsis, and he moves instinctively away from him when he translates for me. I don't know Ignace as well as Innocent does, but I don't think he's any worse than the others.

Driven from the Gitarama region by famine, Ignace settled in Kibungo in the 1970s, working first as a mason before he began clearing farmland. He quickly prospered and grew rich. He branched out into tobacco and coffee, considering those crops a risk worth taking. A tireless worker in his fields, a tough business-man, a strict husband and father, he was hard on his wife, his sons, his day workers. His character was already setting him apart: he was feared and envied. People say that on Sundays, at the hour for Mass, he used to show up in Kibungo in a striped suit with pockets overflowing with money to buy chickens or have a kid slaughtered, which he would take back to his wife to be roasted, and that he'd stuff himself until evening, swilling cans of *urwagwa*.

He also had a reputation for creating scenes. In *cabarets*, Ignace never missed a chance to provoke Tutsis with threats and promises of their approaching doom. He had soaked up anti-Tutsi rancor in his youth, having lived some thirty years on a plot of barren land during the reign of the last Tutsi *mwami*; and like many Hutus of his generation, he blamed the Tutsi kings for the poverty he still remembers with humiliation.

Today, he grumbles more than his colleagues and sneers at their pretense of contrition; he even named his last son Habyari-mana, after the slain Hutu president, because he doesn't give a damn about his reputation. Just to be cheeky, or perhaps with conscious irony, he now walks with the staff of a Tutsi herdsman and is raising two Ankole cows and their calves in a pen behind his house. He doesn't hesitate to share a bottle at Fifi's, sitting in the middle of a bench full of survivors. With the common sense of fatalism, he broods most over his own fate, fulminating against those who dragged him into defeat.

One day he observed, "We said we were working for good: our own good, obviously, the good of the Hutus. Time now points its finger at us for the evil we did to the Tutsis. The defeat changed famous patriots into infamous criminals. That's history, life-size. It's a big mistake not to have heard it knocking at the door."

Pushing your way through the reeds at the lower edge of Ignace's property will bring you to the juncture of the Nyabarongo and Akanyaru rivers, where the Akonakamashyoza, a small island of reeds, seems to float in the riverine mist. This is the island, fabled in Tutsi mythology, that Rwandans hope to include one day in a hypothetical tourist attraction visiting the sources of the Nile.[*]

Meanwhile, black pirogues glide over the calm water, poled along by Tutsi cattlemen fetching heaps of aquatic fodder for the cows lowing hungrily on the riverbank, or by Hutu fishermen bringing their catch to their wives, who will smoke the fish before selling them in the little market of Kibungo.

This market is held in the late afternoon, at the far end of the main village street. Aside from some rare kitchen-garden vegetables like tomatoes or pumpkins (hardly more appreciated than the fish: as so often in Africa, it's meat or nothing), there are candles, cans of oil, and sachets of salt. Nothing really explains the crowd gathered there except the music: from cassette players sitting on the ground pours Congolese soukous, the protean, hip-swinging music that began as a kind of Congolese rumba in the 1930s and spread all over Africa. It's a Hutu market, where young people in jerseys embossed with the names of soccer stars like Diarra,

---

[*] *According to Rwandan legend, this is where the two sacred tributaries of the White Nile mingle and where two processions were held on the day after the death of the reigning monarch: the procession of the Living King, the heir, walking in the sunlight, followed by the procession of the Mummy, the dead king, in the moonlight. —Translator's note*

Ronaldinho, and Cissé hang out among the farm women and their husbands, many of them recently released from Rilima, who don't dare join in the laughter or dancing.

Far from the music, the Tutsis assemble at the other end of the long strip of ground. They're quieter but no less busy in the drinking department. The herds are coming up from their pastures, heading through the village to the clearings where they will spend the night guarded by boys. Chattering off in the distance, like an echo, are turtledoves, cuckoos, and, if one draws close enough to hear them, the fauna of the marshes.

In Kibungo, two hundred kilometers from the equator and perched at an altitude of 1,400 meters, the nights fall early and are cool when they aren't cold and wet during the height of the rainy season. Fifi and Francine light kerosene lamps; charcoal braziers glow here and there on the street and in the courtyards. As bottles of alcohol pass slowly around, a light buzz joins the fatigue that falls at the end of a long day.

This is the moment when some people head home to rest. Others take advantage of the twilight to make their discreet appearance, like Rose, Adalbert's mama, who hardly ever leaves her property anymore in broad daylight, either from uneasiness since her son fled to the suburbs of Kigali, or fury at those who now accuse him all the more loudly.

The townspeople talk about their pastures; voices may be raised on the subject of school fees or some business about trees cut down without the owner's knowledge, but no one argues anymore about what happened in the past. It's also the moment for "hush-hush" gossip, and the hush of silence.

IT'S NOT FAIR

On Tuesday morning, it's *gaçaça* in Nyamata, and there's no sign of life on the main street: padlocks on the shop doors, taxi-buses all parked; only the schoolchildren seem to be awake. Even the religious sects don't dare defy the authorities' instructions. All around, in the fields, on the paths, no one disturbs the atmosphere of abandonment except the boys watching their herds.

The *gaçaça* of the Kayumba neighborhood is held near the secondary school of the APEBU (Association des Parents pour l'Éducation au Bugesera); the one in Kibungo is over by a church meadow; the tribunal in Ntarama meets in a pretty clearing across from the memorial; in Mayange everyone assembles under the only trees on its dusty plain, in the same spot where the humanitarian agencies distribute their aid packages.

In this setting, on a long table placed in the shade of a majestic *umuniyinya* tree, lie piles of dossiers around which five people solemnly take their seats. Over here, that's Benoît with his wide-brimmed hat; there, that's Consolée Murekatete—the wife of the killer Alphonse—who presides over the court. The locals sit in groups of friends and acquaintances. The men are usually in field clothes, except when they expect to participate; the women swaddle their babies in *pagnes* on their backs or cuddle them to their breasts at the first whimper of impatience.

In Kinyarwanda, *gaçaça* means "soft grass," on which Rwandan villagers used to sit in a circle beneath the branches of the *umuniyinya*, the revered "palaver tree," when they had tribal judicial proceedings. This custom goes back to the first Tutsi kings in the sixteenth century, and for four hundred years these "people's courts" dispensed justice—as in many countries in black Africa, moreover—until the introduction of colonial courtrooms. Then they remained active in the villages for minor disputes (over boundaries of a field, the evaluation of a dowry, damage caused by livestock) or when the problem was too delicate to be put before magistrates: acts of sorcery, adultery, illegal labor.

In the time of the Tutsi *mwami*, after the assembled crowd had questioned the plaintiffs, the village chief delivered his verdict. "From as far back as the elders tell it," Innocent explains, "in the spirit of that time, the verdicts of a *gaçaça* were not supposed to be imperious or crushing but to promote reconciliation. Except for cow stealing, obviously. And only the king could pass a sentence of death."

In 1998, in the Hôtel Urugwiro, ministers and jurists began meeting to discuss the insoluble problems of justice posed by the crimes of the genocide four years earlier. In effect, the Rwandan judicial system had been shattered during the killings and the Hutu exodus: tens of thousands of prisoners were huddled in penitentiaries, millions of people were living at liberty on the hills but under constant threat of accusation and punishment, while thousands of survivors waited desperately for some semblance of justice.

During those meetings the idea of reviving the *gaçaça* tradition took root, with these theoretical objectives: the end of impunity; national reconciliation; collective Rwandan participation in the search for justice. Beginning in 2001, *gaçaça* committees were formed with nineteen elected members, called *inyangamugayo*, or "persons of integrity," who received brief but intensive training as judges.

In Nyamata the first stage, the gathering of evidence, began one year later with assemblies every Thursday morning. Marie-Louise Kagoyire was one of those who "didn't want to miss a single word," as she put it. "I'd arrive at eight o'clock. And I listened: the killers' names, where people were cut, all the details about the murder of my husband, Léonard Rwerekana. Each of the killers spoke only a tiny truth, since they were under no obligation, but still, they told a small useful part. For us, that was already something unhoped for."

On the other hand, Claudine Kayitesi went to only two or three sessions: "I sat on my heels, I heard. Killers were whimpering that they'd stolen a wardrobe and some cooking utensils. That they'd been forced to participate. That they hadn't cut anyone. They hadn't seen anything. They'd mended their ways. Hadn't even struck a cow. And were unhappy and unlucky. I waited to be questioned, I gave my answers, I said my eyes had seen hardly anything, I left. On the second day, a well-known Hutu, Aldo Moro, called out, 'Well, if you allow me a little time, I'll reveal a great truth to you.' He stood straight up in the crowd: 'Here are the ones who were beside me during the killings.' And he pointed to a colleague: 'You, stand up like me, because you were definitely with me.' And to another: 'You, too, on your feet, you were also with me,' and he pointed out all the Hutus, one after the other. A great uproar seized the assembly as threats, shouts, laughter burst out on all sides. Then we all left. I decided not to go again. Me, I live in Kanzenze; the path is too long for this kind of nonsense."

Engelbert Munyambonwa attended only one gathering: "I would have liked to learn who killed my sister, and especially where her bones are. But the liars muddled everything up. I felt scorned and baffled once again; I went away for good. I personally was in the mire up to my neck, and something strange and lost comes over me whenever I hear those killers speak."

Old Ignace doesn't feel strange and lost at the trials, just uncomfortable. "Before my release from prison, I was severely advised to give up a bit of the truth at the *gaçaças*. Once a week, I go. I've told about our expeditions twice, a little. Saying more, you can provoke a colleague who will implicate you. Saying less, you can aggravate a Tutsi who will accuse you. You must tiptoe through the details and bow your head while awaiting questions."

A joke is going around the country. During a trial, a survivor accuses a man of joining in a massacre. The man denies this. A second survivor rises to charge him with the same crimes. He denies them. A third accuser, a fourth, cannot manage to shake him. Angrily, the presiding judge addresses him: "Tell me, how many times are you still going to deny the evidence and flout this court?" Turning toward the judge, the accused replies, "You're asking me? You know perfectly well, since you were with me that day!"

Some gatherings drag out in monotonous monologues, whereas other meetings unleash confrontations of startling violence, psychodramas, nervous breakdowns, provoking gestures of both kindness and rage. In the northern and western regions of Rwanda, where the Tutsis, already a tiny minority before the genocide, now find themselves even more isolated, the *gaçaças* sometimes become cruel farces. A team of Hutus, machetes on their shoulders, goes to visit a family on the eve of their deposition, or a struggling and impoverished widow trades her "forget-fulness" for some bags of beans. Sometimes a foreigner is astonished by the arrogance of the judges, dumbfounded by the way the crowd jeers at the demented raving of the elderly or the humiliated confusion of young women. Elsewhere—in Nyamata, for example, where the Tutsi population can withstand the shock—the sessions take a better turn.

In Nyamata, the man presiding over the *gaçaça* is André Kamanda, a law professor who belongs to the generation of brainy, dogmatic Anglophone technocrats who came home from exile in the wake of the Patriotic Front troops right after the end of the genocide—men like the current mayor, police chief, public prosecutor, and local army commander. After three years of judicial inquiries beneath the trees, André Kamanda has compiled ten thousand dossiers detailing offenses ranging from the theft of sheet metal to the massacre of fifty people, and these have resulted in about fifty prison sentences.

"Most Hutus are negationists," according to Alphonse Hitiyaremye. "Not one in a hundred admits the truth. That's understandable. But if they agree to a little participation and make some part a sincere confession, they walk away from the path to prison. In the *gaçaças*, the major role is played by the prisoners released by presidential decree. They want to show their gratitude to the state, and they enjoy denouncing comrades who made fun of them when they were stuck in prison."

And justice? Does the idea of what is right surface in this flood of passionate or calculating evidence? What legality can be created by these populist courts, largely outside the supervision of professional judges? What can these millions of the accused and their accusers expect in the way of simple fairness?

.   .   .

Alphonse Hitiyaremye: "We received a free pardon more than a punishment, because the pardon was more necessary in the country's new situation, given the war, the fields lying fallow, hunger, and the problems raised by wives left on their own.

"The state had determined that many were involved in carrying out the killings without being involved in a deeper ideology, and that it's better to condemn the former government instead of the farmers turned killers. The state believes that the farmers have kept a little innocence after all and are more useful in their fields."

Ignace Rukiramacumu: "The prison time served is not anywhere near the killings committed. Shooting us all? Not an easy thing. Feeding us in Rilima and getting nothing in return seemed too expensive when famine hit the hills. The authorities thought, If they stay eating in prison while the fields return to bush, if the survivors find no food to buy and no good workers for their own land, and if families cry famine in the drought, it will be disastrous. Reconciliation naturally promotes the sowing of every productive field."

Élie Mizinge: "Cutting people with machetes, without any provocation. Without wondering why we're cutting them. Without asking ourselves what it means to cut so many people like that. It's a turbulence of the mind that cannot be judged. Faced with such culprits, justice cannot exact anything fitting except through killing or pardoning. Me, I was spared in the aftermath, I was imprisoned, and later I was released. I was bad, I am nice, I shall be a model of behavior. I shall follow my opportunity without one misstep until God's judgment."

Marie-Louise Kagoyire: "They judged some criminals in the courts. That represents a fraction of the killers, but still, one frac-

tion. Yes, after the genocide there is a justice, but of reconciliation. It adjusts to the numbers of judges, killers, and victims; it
punishes the guilty and prevents vengeance; it proves lenient to
the killers and profitable for the welfare of the country. It fosters
a good outlook for the future. It satisfies the authorities, the
international donors, and as for the sorrow of the survivors, that's
just too bad."

Claudine Kayitesi: "In the courts injustice gobbles up justice.
Obviously, not every killer deserves execution—but still, some of
them, after all. Those who burned babies alive, who cut and
cut till their arms ached, who led expeditions of a thousand
hunters—those should really have disappeared from our lives.
The state has decided to save them. If someone had asked for my
opinion? I would have sent the propagandists and the major leaders to the firing squad. That wasn't done; foreigners exerted
influence, and the authorities proved flexible to favor national
reconciliation. For us, it becomes impossible to relieve our grief,
even with full bellies. Basically, justice is not worrying about the
feelings of survivors."

Berthe Mwanankabandi: "What's the use of looking for mitigat-
ing circumstances for people who butchered day after day after
day and even on Sundays with their machetes? What can you
mitigate? The number of victims? The methods of hacking? The
killers' laughter? Delivering justice would mean killing the killers.
But that would be like another genocide, and would bring chaos.
Killing or punishing the guilty in some suitable way: impossible.
Pardoning them: unthinkable. *Being just* is inhuman.

"Justice finds no place after a genocide, because it surpasses
human intelligence. Priority must be given to the fields, the harvests, the country, and so to the killers as well and to their fami-

lies, who are many and strong. What would become of a nation lying fallow, without schools or sturdy houses, eyed greedily by neighboring countries? This is not a human justice, it's a politics of justice. We can only regret that they never show either sincerity or sorrow."

Innocent Rwililiza: "Justice comes through the application of law, and the law would bring the country to its knees. One-fiftieth of the culprits were punished in some way, and the nation cannot bear any more. When a killer is granted a pardon in the name of reconciliation, neither he nor those around him nor the relatives of his victims feel justice has been served.

"This frustration, for the Tutsis, or this impunity, for the Hutus, will transmit itself in a hideous secret from family to family, generation to generation, and corrupt future life on the hills. For the present, though, it's good. Survivors complain about injustice, but they can understand that they will thereby gain something in return: a sense of security and a full belly. Rising up in vengeance, with your hand trembling from fear and hunger, you cannot win.

"We can't demolish a Hutu society of more than six million people who work hard, behaving humbly and obediently, in order to satisfy a few hundred thousand weak and unstable survivors who grumble and will disappear, as survivors, with the next generation.

"And then there is a truth that has been somewhat disguised: if we, the survivors, obtain neither justice nor reparations, while the prisoners are released after being so copiously fed by the international organizations, it's because we are turning a slightly deaf ear to any words of reconciliation."

SOME SORCERY

Working the land is a hard, grim business, as Jean-Baptiste Murangira has bitterly discovered since his release from the penitentiary in Rilima. He is all the more unhappy in that before the genocide, he never doubted for a moment that his comfortable social position would protect him forever from the misery of famine. The son of a prosperous Hutu family, he had joined the civil service as chief census supervisor in the commune of Nyamata after receiving his high school diploma in the humanities. He wore a neatly ironed shirt and sharply creased trousers at work every day. He acquired some fertile land in Rugunga and hired day workers to tend it. He married a Tutsi, Spéciose Mukandahunga, with whom he settled into a brick "semi-durable" house on a slope of Ntarama Hill, where all the Tutsi families welcomed him cordially.

During the killings, his two chief concerns were to save his Tutsi wife from his colleagues' machetes and to be a credit to his social position. He succeeded on both counts, thanks to his exploits on the expeditions, which were adequate if not enthusiastic, according to witnesses at the time.

Upon his return from Congo in the autumn of 1996, anticipating that he would be arrested, Jean-Baptiste went of his own accord to the prosecutors in Nyamata to offer scraps of confessions, which might be read as regrets, remorse, opportunism, or all of the above. The tribunal sentenced him to fifteen years in prison, which did not discourage his campaign for atonement. In Rilima penitentiary he recovered his former privileges in a way, since he immediately became the leader of a government-sponsored association of repentant detainees, whose members included the rest of the Kibungo gang. His objective was to legitimize the successive waves of discharges that were to begin in January 2003, and he became one of the first prisoners released. After his stint in the reeducation camp in Bicumbi, where he proved a model student, Jean-Baptiste returned in the company of Pio to his hill, Ntarama, to see the family from whom he'd heard no news while imprisoned in Rilima.

The first surprise awaiting him delights him no end: he finds his wife, Spéciose, working in their field, which she has neither sold nor subdivided, and without any lover or illegitimate children loitering in the vicinity.

After a moment of relief, the bad news overwhelms him. Although his wife has managed to preserve the land, to survive during his years of imprisonment she has had to abandon their house in Ntarama along with all their possessions, taking refuge in a rudimentary sheet-metal adobe once inhabited by farm-workers. What's more, several children have vanished without a trace, while others waste no time in upbraiding their father, reproaching him for his crimes, especially since he can no longer pay the school fees indispensable for their education. And finally, his collaboration with the judicial system does not win over his Tutsi neighbors, unimpressed by his repentance.

Banished for good from public office, too poor to start up a small business, Jean-Baptiste finds himself with a hoe on his shoulder, drawn down the path to his field by his wife and eldest son, who have been trudging along that path for eight years.

Up at five, sorghum porridge, hoeing, weeding, planting in withering heat or pouring rain—the earth is unforgiving to the neophyte. Each time we meet, Jean-Baptiste has crumpled a bit more; his palms are cracking, his hair growing grizzled, his voice turning plaintive. Gone, those morning coffees while listening to the radio, relaxing in his courtyard until office hours began; gone, the Sunday roasts, the white shirts, the beers with pals in the *cabaret*, the official openings, the wedding invitations.

The harshness of his labors does not change his behavior, however. Like other former prisoners, Jean-Baptiste has no intention of apologizing to the families of his victims, although his reluctance doubtless stems more from fear than from cynicism; he will stick to his calculated confessions. On the other hand, he participates eagerly in the politics of reconciliation, just as he'd devoted time in prison to his association of repentant detainees. He never misses a reconciliation meeting, renews his penitence, offers his testimony. Friendly greetings pour from his lips at casual encounters on the path to the church and in the center of Ntarama, where his neighbors, finally losing the battle, take pity on him and let him slip back into the company of the circulating *urwagwa* bottle. As the *gaçaças* draw near, he does not shy away. Less talkative than Léopord Twagirayezu, more zealous than the rest of the band, he holds steady, minimizes his role, plays defense with his own dossier to exonerate himself, but inventories the expeditions with precision and energetically denounces his accomplices.

One morning Jean-Baptiste goes down to the field as usual. With the first stroke of the hoe, a blinding pain streaks along his spine; his knees buckle at the shock, tipping him over on his side, where he begins to sweat and rave deliriously. His wife and son carry him home to lay him on his bed, where he lies prostrate. At first he thinks it's some form of exhaustion or an attack of malaria, but "later, when I felt the sickness chewing up my skeleton, I recognized its evil ways and knew it was indeed a traditional poisoning."

Poisoning? How? "Here on the Rwandan hills," explains Jean-Baptiste, "these attacks are well known. The offender buries a line of poison on the track the target will take. When this person steps across the line, the poison bites the spine and seeps into the bones." And those who come along afterward? "The first person is the only one aimed at by the poison; the others are spared. It's a very sophisticated spell." Poisoned by whom? "I was getting quite the evil eye from many colleagues as the *gaçaças* approached, because of my evidence and its likely consequences." No evil eye from the Tutsi families of victims? "No: the vengeance of the Tutsis, that would be a huge thing, that could be pandemonium. Answering the killings with death would be too risky for them. No Tutsi would dare consult a poisoner about the genocide—and no poisoner could go through with that."

What does the doctor say? "In Rwanda, if you've been poisoned, it's a waste of money to consult a doctor. He has no idea how to fight off sorcery. Only bush medicine can put you back on your feet. I consulted an old mama with a good reputation for fighting poisons against bones. She looked at me, prodded me, asked me for two thousand francs for the cure. She carefully prepared the magic herbs in the courtyard, along with the secret words."

Despite the healer's efforts, Jean-Baptiste is visibly wasting away: his voice is fading, what few muscles still cling to his bones are atrophying, and he suffers from terrible migraines. He can hardly move and barely sleeps. In the village the prognoses are studies in pessimism (he will/won't make it through the next rainy season), but one cannot say that everyone is saddened by his condition. Three months pass, during which the initial phase of the *gaçaça* courts, the all-important gathering of evidence establishing the lists of suspects, is completed in Ntarama. Meanwhile, the healer's herbs battle the illness in Jean-Baptiste's body. To the astonishment of those around him, one fine day he manages to sit up, then essays a few shaky steps with a walking stick, watched by his dumbfounded spouse.

Spéciose, a valiant worker, has taken up the hoe again with a will. A solitary, dignified woman and a devoted mother, she never weeps over her fate. Rejected by one side because of her Tutsi blood—for many, the cause of all the recent misfortunes—and by the other side because she was saved by her Hutu husband, at the cost of her relatives' blood, she inspires suspicion and feels herself rebuffed, pushed back deep into her field, so she protects herself from everyone and hardly ever speaks anymore. Nevertheless, chatting as she escorts us to our car after a visit we've just paid to Jean-Baptiste, she ventures a suggestion with a faintly ironic smile.

"From now on destiny presents itself in camouflage: perhaps the poison actually saved him from a much worse fate. Maybe Jean-Baptiste really ought to live again in the penitentiary in Rilima . . . To escape the evil eye behind thick walls, to defend himself against backbiting rumors. To put distance between himself and accusations and let his wrongdoing sleep, and afterward, to bring back to his land a farmer's brave strength and the necessary vigor of a real husband in good health."

CONSOLÉE, DISGUSTED

One morning three years ago, while we were sitting in the prison administrator's garden in Rilima discussing the attitude of Hutu women during the massacres, Alphonse differed with his colleagues by setting his wife apart from other women: "My wife used to tell me, 'Listen, really, going every day, every day, it's too much. This filthiness should be stopped' . . . Toward the end she refused to share the bed, she slept on the ground, she said, 'You are cutting so many, you cannot count them anymore. I am afraid of this foul thing. You are turning into an animal, and I won't sleep with an animal.' "

Intrigued by this act of rebellion, unimaginable in the terrifying atmosphere of that time, I was eager to meet the lady, Consolée Murekatete. But I could not visit her at home until after Alphonse was released, because all the Hutu women followed a strict law of silence throughout the detention of their men.

The couple's house is beside the Nyamata road, which follows and overlooks the course of the Nyabarongo River, whose waters nourish a tropical flora more lush than the vegetation of Kibungo. I go out there on a stifling day and find Consolée in her yard, where she and her son are shelling beans by beating the pods with long sticks, in a kind of dance with a rhythm and breadth of movement that are both magnificent and exhausting. Alphonse, meanwhile, in the coolness of his room, is weighing and bagging a heap of grain.

Streaming with sweat, Consolée stops to offer me hospitality in a living room currently chock-full of sacks. After chatting for a few moments about beans, children, and the *gaçaça* court over which she presides in this sector, we turn to the killing time and her quarrels with Alphonse.

Unsurprisingly, she says she feels awkward addressing the subject and does not confirm her rebellion, yet she answers unflinchingly in spite of herself: "After a whole day combing the marshes, Alphonse stank too much of blood and mire. That reeking odor could provoke great fear, but nothing could be done about it. Keeping one's husband at arm's length, that's too serious in Africa. Opposing him in those days could be a cutting offense. We did have to have some married intimacy, after all, but it was no longer the same. There was a change: it was a bit forced, but since he was my husband, I could do nothing but accept him if he was hot."

Then she adds, "To tell you the truth, myself, I don't see any great disagreement between the Hutu men and women during those tumultuous days. The men cut zealously in the marshes; the women burned with the same zeal in pillaging the fields and houses. I can certainly tell you, without dodging around, about the lives of the killers' wives."

I encourage her all the more sincerely to do so because I have run up against a wall of denial from almost all the Hutu women—and the young Hutus as well, who were children or adolescents during the killings and have been "tetanized" by the possible effects of their words, the threats these might provoke, and by a vague feeling of guilt, thus leaving only the Hutu men to tell the story in their own way.

. . .

Consolée Murekatete: "The atmosphere broke down the day of the plane crash. People coming and going, young men running along the paths; people were no longer moving forward with a sure footing. Like a bird, the good understanding of old had flown away. On the third day the authorities whistled up an assembly in the center of Nyamabuye. The men set out on the first expedition and came back that afternoon, laughing. They were clapping and singing. It was like a wedding festivity, except for their muddy farmers' work pants. They left quite early every morning, singing to boost their morale, give themselves courage. And they were also clearly singing for happiness at this new life opening up. Alphonse would leave with the others. For him it was joy and excitement. He had changed completely since abandoning farming: he forgot his cares, he never even looked at his field anymore.

"So at noon in the village center, the usual people were gone, since the expeditions took longer than the morning fieldwork. Evenings, we prepared food at the ordinary time, except that meals were obviously more copious, thanks to the slaughtering of the cows. Husbands and wives celebrated; everyone was drinking, talking, singing some more. We ate meat, too much meat, sometimes even leaving some on the grills. Many men piled up money through their looting skills. They negotiated, stocked up, sold drinks to colleagues who cared nothing for commerce and felt rich enough as it was. And people got drunk—men, women, even the children found themselves invited.

"When the men were out hunting, the women remained quietly stunned. Mistrust settled in. We stayed home, hardly ever leaving the yard except to draw water. Two or three families might gather in one another's home to talk about what was sweeping over the hill, but there was no more walking around as before. If you had to go a long distance to fetch seeds or get news, you had to be accompanied by a man. We were protecting ourselves against danger, basically, without knowing what it was.

"Women are not born for this kind of killing. Changes in their domestic routines can upset them, and they saw less promise in the new situation. Still, they didn't all react in the same way. Some seemed quite pleased, because their husbands were bringing back loot and plenty of food in the evening; such women saw the recent turn of events as a stroke of good fortune, and they adjusted easily to the windfalls. Some women went off on little forays to plunder Tutsis hiding in houses or the bush, or to pillage goods before their husbands found them, and then hide such thefts away. Others, envious, might exchange bitter words. Those who found more might share with those who got less, depending on each woman's character.

"But frankly, one never heard a pitying word for the Tutsi women who had been our neighbors. No complaint from wives about the Tutsi women our husbands might be raping—as long as our men performed their dirty deeds in the papyrus of the marshes, sheltered from prying eyes and gossiping tongues.

"Some women, though, were saddened by this changing life. Personally, I was a little afraid. Too much blood unnerved me. I could see that sooner or later a punishment would arise, so I was always on guard. But we were obliged to obey, that's normal. No woman could contradict her husband or she would get a tougher beating than usual. Alphonse would come home in the evening quite worked up. He didn't behave at all badly with me; he didn't yell and scream as some of the men did at their wives. But he talked in an alarming way. He wasn't nice anymore; he smelled of death and Primus. He behaved brutally in everything. He was throwing all his farmer's habits into the ditch. His hand never let go of the machete; his mind was turning away from wisdom. So I had constantly to be careful, careful.

"After our return from the camps in Congo, life back home took its revenge. Alphonse was not expected to ever leave Rilima. I had nothing. A Tutsi family had taken over our land for two years and our goods had been stolen. So I would go offer my arms to Tutsi families in exchange for a little food. Many Tutsi families of the diaspora had returned from abroad with money and were acquiring the lands of those who had disappeared. The times were profitable for them: they bought plots of land, they hired the labor offered them. We did not speak to one another. Fear dogged us; we wiped away the spit and insults of others. There was no lack of biting quarrels among Hutu women, either: jealousy ricocheted among us, because some women saw their men leave for the fields every morning, while others visited theirs in prison—men who were no worse than the farmers at home. One visit to Rilima meant two days of walking and waiting.

"Alphonse had changed when he came out of prison. His body was frailer; his spirit was subdued, worried. He had been the richest man in Nyamabuye, and nostalgia for his losses clouded his mind. Today, when life seems more clement, he has become quite nice again. Fieldwork and married life seem as before, except for the fatigue of age, obviously. We shall never again enjoy abundance but can live together acceptably. I won't forget the lesson I have learned. Man cannot be trusted. The image I will keep of him is unimaginable wickedness."

DARK VISIONS OF AFRICA

How many white writers, upon returning from that continent, have not dreamed they had written *Out of Africa*?*
What pride, upon awakening, to have been even briefly the author of this masterpiece; and above all, what a lovely illusion to have dreamily experienced, like Karen Blixen, those years of ineffable grace in Africa, a time made precious by the understanding she shared with Africans, the happiness she found in the Kenya of those days, and the harmony between the people and their country, with its unforgettable landscapes, animals, and the pungent scents of that ancient land: an improbable idyll that vanishes with the morning light and into the pages of pastoral literature.

Over the years, my travels in Africa have persuaded me that one of the most deeply rooted misunderstandings between Africans and Westerners, doubtless dating from their first encounter, probably springs from the different ways in which they view change.

The white man has an atavistic, passionate, and even feverish desire for change. He has hardly slipped behind the wheel of his

---

* *In her memoir* Out of Africa *(1973), about life on her coffee plantation in Kenya, Isak Dinesen (nom de plume of the Danish baroness Karen von Blixen-Finecke) celebrated the Africans' closeness to nature because she believed it kept them in touch with an original, Edenic "truth" of being that modern cultures elsewhere had lost, a divergence she saw as the root of a fundamental difference between the African and Western ways of reconciling modernization with nature. —Translator's note*

new Peugeot 307 when he begins eagerly awaiting the unveiling of the 308. As an adolescent, he fantasizes about changing the world—his world, at least. At the beach he looks forward to vacationing soon in the mountains. If he's a chef, he rearranges his menu every six months. Newly married, he begins thinking about acquiring a mistress. A rancher strives to breed a better strain of cattle. A mother doesn't raise her youngest child the way she did her firstborn. After a third defeat, a sports manager changes half the players on his roster and the other half at the end of the season. The sacred rituals of fashion and the bulimia of technology are among the symptoms of this obsession with change. Whether it's winning or losing, the West likes to change its team.

The African, on the contrary, resists such change, even if the team is in trouble. The Peugeot 504 was beloved in Africa: this "desert camel" was robust, reliable, good-looking, and above all perfectly suited to its job, so 504 fans still speak of it with nostalgia, wondering why it was retired (in 1983 in Europe, in 2005 in Nigeria). Even today Africans miss the valiant 404 bush taxi used in the 1960s and 1970s, and with good reason. A stockbreeder of zebu cattle, a beast acclimated to its environment since the dawn of time, distrusts the new crossbreeds recommended by agricultural experts. The African eats his spicy *mafé* peanut stew or lemony chicken *yassa* with the same pleasure every single day. He extols the traditional hierarchical family, believes the radio more than television, pays closer attention to village elders and griots, those tribal musicians and oral historians, than he does to any dynamic young cadres, and clings confidently to age-old laws and traditions, which he doesn't try to bend or bypass. He worries more about water than about gas. Be he a government minister or an entertainment star, he returns to his village to visit his family and check on his little patch of land.

Yet, the African, nomadic in origin and a great traveler under the gaze of God, fears neither movement nor novelty. He is naturally communicative and polyglot. As an emigrant, he adapts to his new—perhaps even hostile—environment and demonstrates astonishing intelligence in any unfamiliar situation. His flexible mind sometimes assimilates a technological innovation by leaping over many of its interim stages. Over a few months in Nyamata, people went directly from the single crackling colonial public telephone in the post office, where they waited hours for their turn to experience a fairly inaudible communication lasting only a few seconds, to cell phones and e-mail, thus skipping landline phones, faxes, answering machines, and Minitels. Which doesn't bother them, but their new technology doesn't particularly fascinate or thrill them, either.

The *pagne* is an African invention, and you'd be hard-pressed to find a more ingenious one. The *pagne* is the colorful sheet on which Africans sleep, in which they roll themselves up on cold nights. It's a towel after ablutions, the skirt one wraps about one's hips upon awakening, the shawl across the shoulders in the rainy season. The *pagne* is a baby backpack for mothers, and it ties up bundles for going into town or on a long trip. *Pagnes* are spread out on the ground when women get together to chat, and hung over windows at siesta time.

Pagnes are the mainstay of trousseaux, accompanying refugees to the camps and immigrants to their new homes. In the West they flower on the streets of African immigrant neighborhoods in the spring and embellish souvenir photos at international conferences. As gifts, they are always welcome: beautiful, inexpensive, strong, and suitable for any purpose you desire. And yet, they cannot prevent the invasion of the "Made in China" suits, tailored dresses, handbags, suitcases, curtains, baby strollers, rugs, and napkins that are spreading throughout African markets.

I had a very good friend in Nyamata, Dr. Georges Magera. After brilliant medical studies in Paris and Prague, he trundled his medical bag around almost all of Africa, notably in Kinshasa, where for many years he was one of the seven personal physicians of President Mobutu, an experience that furnished him with sidesplitting jokes and anecdotes. Back in his homeland and suffering from a throat tumor that made swallowing painful, Dr. Magera decided to subsist exclusively on beer, which he drank all day long. His thinness and tremors were equaled only by his kindness and sense of humor. He went on managing the region's only hospital, setting all fractures, bringing bushels of babies into the world, and fighting malaria epidemics at the back of beyond in the bush.

One evening, on the pretext that he'd been invited to a wedding the following Saturday, Dr. Magera borrowed my jacket. As it happened, he went off with it in his coffin not long after that. As he was trying it on, though, he said, "You see, this whole world is divided between the tailored and the draped. Myself, I'd lean more toward the tailored, but it's such bullshit when they keep trying to shove that down everyone else's throats."

And so the traveler in Africa comes to believe that the Western fascination with change is what prevents this continent from accepting it. Africa rejects the West's narrow conception of modernity and can't adjust to the accelerations and sudden turns it imposes. And, like any person constrained to follow an unavoidable course of action, Africa naturally dillydallies and reacts inopportunely, making the wrong choices, giving in to poor impulses, unable to resist the temptation now and again of tossing the cards up in the air, since it feels it cannot win the game or won't even be allowed to play. This sense of exclusion creates confusion among the peoples of Africa, who seek certainty and serenity by turning to religious sects, ethnic groups, and local dialects, and by taking refuge in various "home fronts" that foment violence at the slightest outside threat.

Whatever the nature of this dismay, it springs from a sense of rejection by the modern world, the impossibility of feeling at ease there. It provokes riots, clashes, destruction, recurrent massacres, and metastasizing wars. And you'd almost think it might infect Africa with a kind of virus of self-destruction, of which the Tutsi genocide would be the extreme manifestation.

But up on the hills of Nyamata, do they share that impression?

First of all, how do they see their Africa, and in what way do they see themselves as African? How do they look at us? Do they feel unfortunate, misunderstood, unloved, manipulated? How do they experience that latent attraction/revulsion they feel for the Western world? Do they think their current troubles are only temporary, the necessary result of wrenching adjustments at too brutal a pace? Or do they fear this change will prove fatal? Do they feel they are living in a chaotic period of transition, or a tragedy of abandonment?

Innocent Rwililiza: "Saying that Africa is an underprivileged or disadvantaged continent is just ridiculous. More than anything else, Africa is the cradle of humanity! It's a huge thing to have produced the ancestors of *all* Homo sapiens and the roots of knowledge, here in the birthplace of every civilization in the world. That was really Africa's chance to get out in front and offer its philosophy to the planet, and no one robbed us of our chance—we simply lost it.

"Next, Africa's climate is blessed like no other on earth. The soil is bursting with fertility, the sunshine plentiful, the rains come: you plant the seed and the sapling springs up. You eat your fill. An African always feels pretty happy in the morning: nature has spoiled us. We haven't had to fight like the Chinese or the Germans up north against cold, snow, hunger, overpopulation, pollution, all those calamities. It's our ambitions that have suffered; we've lost the habit of tackling adversity. An African doesn't feel outdone in intellectual research: Africans learn quickly, probably much more quickly than others. It's not ideas or courage we lack, but tenacity. And the closer we live to the equator, the more easygoing we are; it's not polite to say so, but us, we know it, it's obvious.

"In Africa, democracy is gaining, coups d'état are thinning out, children fill the benches in school, believers enjoy their religions. Many Africans go abroad, where they adopt European or American customs, returning with a modern outlook and technological finds, inventions such as computers. Africans are finding more and more favor in the eyes of Whites, who seem pleased and willing to hand over money. Still, Africans do feel they're under the thumb of humanitarian aid organizations, the World Bank loans, and the programs of the International Monetary Fund. The lucky ones seize the chance to enrich themselves, the unlucky grow poorer in the lower classes, and everyone envies the Whites. Frankly, our modernization? We copy it from the Whites—economic planning, computerization, democratization—and harm our own civilization, because we are so lacking in major areas, like technologies. Africans learn all the technological tricks, comply with international standards, take advantage of subsidies, muttering all the while that they don't want any more help; they're tired of taking orders from Whites, and they can't wait to get out of their own country.

"When all this bothers them too much, they get angry, but they don't dare bellyache about it. They mutter, can't bring themselves to air their grievances, and then one day they go on a rampage, killing one another, looting, wreaking havoc, because they kept their dissatisfaction locked up too long in their hearts. It's a day of wrath. And on top of that, they're destroying their own possessions, the things they need, because after all, they haven't the strength to go let off steam and smash everything in some other country, as the Americans or Europeans do. Africans apply savagery and brutality at home to solve their problems.

"The White? His role in Africa is to assist and exploit. He sells cars with tinted windows, puts up frighteningly tall multi-story buildings, invites us to his universities, spends millions of dollars to prevent AIDS, irrigates kilometers of plantations. I don't know if he's the friend or enemy of the Blacks. The White is strict, well organized, and secretly very, very crafty. The African plants a seed in the ground and is content with what grows. The White, he digs beneath the seed to rip out a diamond or phosphates and suchlike, and then holds out a little contract.

"The White has no idea how Africans envy him—those in the countryside, at least. And no idea how they fear him. For example, you see a thousand people assembled in a village, with dignitaries, teachers, local bigwigs, well-dressed people with their wives glittering in all their jewelry. Okay: A white man happens by. He's wearing sandals—no socks—and a rumpled shirt and trousers. No one knows what he knows, thinks, or has, but the speaker addressing the crowd still stops talking to watch the White, who will be more respected than anyone else at that meeting until he vanishes down the road.

"Many Blacks seem satisfied with their skin. Many Blacks are uneasy with it. They know that black skin never seems clean enough to white eyes. Blacks joke about it: 'White skin, you wash it, shave it, it's white. Black skin, you spend years scrubbing it and nothing changes. That's why the Whites take us for nice but rather lazy little idiots!' Then laughter all around, another beer, and on to the next joke.

"When the situation gets complicated in Africa, our skin doesn't help, even for us Blacks. In school, for example, every year we're sincerely troubled when the teacher discusses the morphological diversity of the peoples of the world, the great variety of human features. Some young pupils always ask why the Black isn't as carefully put together as the others, with that nose, or hair, or skin. As long as we keep acting like savages now and then with our guns and machetes, those absurd questions will keep doing damage to the mouths of children.

"Myself, I have not traveled. I'm not familiar with foreign customs, except through books or television. As far as I can tell, abroad, it's fine. Here, too, it's fine. What sets African nerves on fire is when the climate changes. When the desert spreads, when the rainy seasons skip their turn, when there aren't enough fields, and foodstuffs sell for too little or cost too much to buy. Africans are more upset by global warming than by the AIDS virus.

"But I don't believe that Africans are discouraged by poverty or frightened by globalization and the like. It's envy, that's the problem. They're plain jealous of their neighbors, city folks, and Whites, and when quarrels heat up, they lose their heads to an anger that smashes everything. Africans don't self-destruct from despair or poverty—not at all. It's greed that sparks the wars. Among the people who make Africa self-destruct, the most telling are the ones who go to Europe or America. They see democracy close up, know all the wily tricks of progress; they amass money, make themselves *très chic*, speak elegantly—and when they come home, they scheme and stir up what's primitive in each of us, to make a profit behind the scenes.

"I know next to nothing about natural disasters in the lands of the Sahel and deserts, countries like Mali or Ethiopia, but I do know that Congo could be more flourishing than Scandinavia, and so could Sierra Leone or the Ivory Coast. Nobody's forcing

Africans to tear one another's guts out over there or anywhere else. There's no catastrophe driving them to trash everything, no dire fate like poverty or injustice or sickness. Just greed. Anyway, the poorest people are never the ones who wreck things: they're way too busy swinging the hoe in their fields or lining up to get bags from the World Food Program.

"In Africa, I love the climate (when it's being nice) and our respect for family. Here we offer hospitality to relatives who come even when they're uninvited and never want to leave. We seek shelter with our big brothers, who help us out, no complaints. We visit back and forth, we share and exchange provisions. We hand a plate to our little sisters and offer a bed to our paternal uncles. It's a very good thing. We watch our children grow up and we make new ones, because we don't know how many will survive the epidemics and we want always to have enough left.

"I also like our *cabarets*. In Africa, when a man doesn't show up at the *cabaret*, we say he's too sick or too poor. We never stop joking around in the *cabarets*; we discuss the world among friends every evening, as if the world were listening in, and it cracks us up. Personally, I'm content like that. But African brotherhood is unreliable. The genocide taught me that Africans show no more fellowship than Whites do. Our brothers in Uganda, Burundi, Congo: what did they do in 1994? We were being hunted through the marshes by our neighbors, butchered with machetes, raped by youths, robbed by children, without receiving a tiny gesture of rescue from the countries around us . . . It's heartbreaking."

Eugénie: "God made me African, and I thank God for that. I believe the advantage of Africa lies in its bountiful crops. Agriculture and stockbreeding: those are Africa's gifts to its people, the chance for a lovely life. Africans work so hard in their fields. When the rains come, when the weather is gentle, everything grows, and they are content. But if the land dries out, they start coveting their neighbors' supplies, and if enough folks heat up, they go to war. War—that scares people more than all the technological jolts from the Whites. And Whites? You never know what they're up to. They're too crafty to show themselves plain. But African leaders—you can hear them breathing anger and hatred into the farmers.

"In Africa, you can escape from your family, your country, your religion, but not your ethnic identity. When an African hears danger rumble and takes fright, he clings to his ancestors, to his hill, to what he's used to, and in the very depths of fear he turns to his ethnic group. That's really your last hope. When war thunders on the horizon, you run to your own people, and that's when you can die in great numbers.

"Me, I was a child who took joy in being Tutsi. Later, in the forest of Kayumba, I found myself cursed for being Tutsi and felt betrayed by life because of my Tutsi blood. Now I'm proud of that blood once again. In spite of everything, I know it holds me prisoner. Africa is vast and it is ancient; the genocide taught me that savagery will always lie in wait there."

Claudine: "Whites say that Africans are incapable of devising a long-term project, of keeping a secret, of sweating in a very systematized kind of work. But in 1994, the Hutus managed all that and handsomely, too, if I may put it that way. They organized exemplary killings. This genocide shows that Africans can work just as well as anyone else when they know that superior interests are at stake.

"Africa is a place of farming and of war. Farming is its fortune, war its misfortune. Off in my *mudugudu*, I can't provide any worthwhile reflections on all the good and bad deeds of the Whites in Africa. Farming and war, however, do indeed hold the destiny of all Africans in their grip. Personally, I don't know what the Whites are up to in these African wars; I've heard that they've encouraged ethnic conflicts—for example, in Rwanda. Still, it was Rwandans who went for their machetes to get rid of other Rwandans: you didn't see a single White raise a blade.

"Rwanda was the little land of a thousand hills; now it's the land of a thousand problems. Before, Rwanda was happier, thanks to our families and neighbors. We farmed pretty fields together, and we shared. When a dispute broke out, our elders stepped in decisively, restoring calm. Whenever reprisals erupted, we rallied. When I was little, we lived more prosperously: food grew abundantly, our health was good, education smiled at us, harvests exceeded our needs, we raised lovely cows. Even the wars held back on their ferocity.

"Nowadays our herds are disappearing for lack of pastureland and because they cause such bad blood with the Hutus. Food crops will vanish for lack of fields. The doors of universities are jammed with would-be students. Nothing seems worthwhile; we distrust the changes offered to us. We feel too befuddled by the enormity of the world and the discoveries of our planet. We still cherish a bit of hope for the children and find the strength to get by, but feel no more pleasure for ourselves, only longing for what is gone, and envy. And that is making us hard.

"Africa is a continent of extremes. There are Africans who are richer than Americans, and others who possess simply some animals and a pair of pants. In Kigali, it seems, Rwandans watch movies on cell phones or computers, but in Kibungo, most of us have never used a telephone or watched a single movie, even on a television. Reason why people's characters are going to extremes. For example, a party is planned for a wedding or baptism. All the neighbors are invited. They dress up, join enthusiastically in the festivities, enjoying themselves, laughing, delighting in the bride's happiness. Things heat up, the jests turn sour, and quarreling breaks out—bickering over livestock or a dowry, quickly shushed by chatting guests. The next day these same people get out their machetes and return with torches to set the house on fire. Boundless greed is to blame.

"Whites speak of poverty, discouragement, or ignorance, but truly it is greed. When they were killing Tutsis, the Hutus did not appear poor, or discouraged, or ignorant. They feared the *inkotanyi*, but more than anything else they were heartened by great hopes for grabbing the country, scooping up the Tutsis' fields and eating their cows.

"Being black is clearly harder than being white—another reason why Blacks seem so unstable. The killings of the genocide are not the only thing that has changed my mind. Africans will share bottles and fine words, then flash into killing one another everywhere—in Congo, Uganda, Burundi. And the Whites, seeing them as savages, hurry to withdraw their good opinion.

"I am myself a Rwandan and I am afraid of Rwandans. I am an African and I am afraid of Africans. Happiness, for an African, it's children first of all. It's having wonderful children all around you, to earn respect, to show your strength. To prepare arms for work, and dowries for the future, and to keep hope alive. In Africa, children are not only riches: they are the last hope—but of what, we no longer know . . . You think of happiness while you watch your little ones grow in good fellowship and health. Happiness, for an African, it's also being welcome in the family, the comfort of neighbors, helping one another for the usual labors and just coping with life. When you offer to pitch in for the harvests. When you can share your worries with a relative or a neighbor. But when your family has been hacked to pieces, when you shake at the thought of your children meeting men on the path, and when you cannot trust those who live close by, what good can you find in Africa? If you hear muttering near the *mudugudu*, if you pick up echoes of distant killings, you lose all peace of mind.

"Personally, I would rather be white—yes, I'd rather have white skin, here in Kanzenze or anywhere else. I say this sincerely. I love my black skin, and that of my husband and children, above all others. To me it is lovely and soft, and I don't find a white appearance more pleasing—quite the contrary. But whiteness is more comfortable, more moderate, more advantageous than blackness."

At that point, a pang of doubt stopped me from continuing this discussion with Claudine. To me it seemed disloyal to Africans—my friends in Bamako or Nairobi, Nouadhibou or Lubumbashi—to keep putting questions about so vast and cosmopolitan a continent to people who had recently survived an ordeal as harrowing as extermination.

A SCAR IMPOSSIBLE TO HIDE

"Life is going well. It's offering me improvements. I've signed up at the training center in Gitarama to learn heavy-vehicle mechanics, because school wasn't working out anymore, on account of my wound. I couldn't manage to memorize anything of what I'd learned the day before. Intense reading gave me awful headaches and a runny nose, and I felt laughed at, so I became aggressive and turned away into loneliness. I'm still an orphan in my aunt's house in Gatare. That can't last, on account of she has a damaged son. My aunt thinks I'm a bit in the way, since I don't do a thing around the house."

That's how Cassius Niyonsaba sums up his latest news for me when I run into him by chance as he walks alone in a meadow by the Nyamata Memorial, housed in the town's former church. He accepts with pleasure when I offer him a Primus in the parish *cabaret*, which is managed by kindly nuns in one of the buildings clustered around the old church. It's cool in the *cabaret*, and the garden out in back, with its pleasant bamboo alcoves, is a favorite spot for a secret rendezvous, protected from eavesdropping by the raucous cackling of the parish chickens.

I first met Cassius seven years earlier, at this same memorial. A child of twelve at the time, he was going there after school to wait for nightfall before heading on home. With a soccer ball parked between his feet, he would lean back against the little wall, facing the rows of carefully lined-up skulls, which he seemed willing to stare at forever. At other times, sitting with the guardian in front of the church, he answered questions from foreign visitors who came out from the capital to pay their respects. He enjoyed telling them how when he was seven years old he managed to escape from the massacre in the church, the sole survivor of his immediate family.

That kid has grown into a tall fellow with a deep voice and big straight shoulders, dressed American-style in spite of the heat: checked shirt, jeans, running shoes. The scar across his scalp, however, is still as chilling as ever.

Cassius retains only four clear images from the killings in the church: "the mama I watched get cut right before my own turn, the machete blade swung up over my head, the hiding place of leaves in the forest where I spent days, and the wound, because it putrefied, so that I still tend to scratch at the insects that were eating my head."

As for the rest—scrambling and shoving, being crushed, the screaming from the trapped crowd, shouting from the throng outside, blows, blood spurting and dripping, then somehow getting out of the church and being helped by a Hutu woman leaning over him in a thicket to give him sips of water—the sequence of events is still confused, and he says, "There's all this uproar in my imagination when the memories crash together." This uproar creates variations in the stories he offers his listeners when he tries to string those memories together and explain, to himself as well as others, how and with whose help he escaped the church and the carnage that dispatched five thousand people there. Horribly wounded, he vanished for several weeks, probably off in a forest, and wound up in an orphanage where his aunt found him three months later. No one has ever been able to help him solve this mystery.*

Cassius does have clear, bright memories of his early childhood: "My parents had sent me as a herd boy to my grandmother in Ntarama. I was used to her and my maternal aunt. We had four big milk cows and some calves. I was clever at keeping ticks off the cows and finding tasty grasses out in the bush. At my grandmother's, the food and clothes, they were good. I loved school without any laziness. It was fun to watch the herds with other kids in the pastureland, on account of we played games like soccer.

"After, the genocide shut me off from childhood. I came to a stop, I missed out. I was blocked off on all sides—from studying, finding myself a family, building a home, getting a proper job. If I can land work as an auto mechanic, I'll get back to a little comfort, but it will still be off to the side. Life . . . I'm dealing with it now, but it does trip me up."

And that is why Cassius no longer tries to fix this "sidelining"; in fact, he takes pleasure in distancing himself from others, in being seen as a loner, and he admits that he now devotes his energy to remembrance of the genocide. Thanks to much listening and reflection, he has learned to tell the story of that cataclysm in polished and sincere words to those who inevitably ask him about it. And he can be quite precise about the aftermath of such an event.

Cassius: "At my age, of course I ought to prefer soccer games, action films, jokes and drinks with friends. But for me, pastimes

---

* In Life Laid Bare, *Cassius explained that he was hit by a hammer in the Nyamata church and then by a machete up in Kayumba Forest, where a Hutu woman found and secretly tended to him. He later learned that her husband, discovering that she had helped a Tutsi child, "killed her with a knife, in one thrust." —Translator's note*

are something different. I think about 1994 every day, especially when I remember how I'm not like everyone else. I think about my hiding place, my wound, my dead family. Enduring all that, it's really something, and I don't want to lose one speck of what happened. I'm interested in documentaries about the genocide, radio programs, the mourning ceremonies, and I like the music they play at commemorations. I do the opposite of the people around me. I feel my loneliness when I go near them, and I change direction when they look too happy.

"I don't have any true friends, except a few survivors here and there with whom I can agree to talk about the genocide. Girls speak to me but not personally at all. I don't feel any attraction to them. I'd rather spend my spare time at the memorial than taking walks to flirt. I'm held tight by a lack of willpower. Girls like fancy talk, but me, I just don't feel in the mood to come up with those clever things and I don't laugh when my companions joke around. Girls, you have to tease them with smart chatter so that they'll agree to keep you company and come visit you. That desire to tease them is something I don't have.

"Still, I do believe that I'll get married someday, out of respect for my parents, on account of I'm the only survivor in my family and I don't want our line to die out. For an African, that would be the deepest shame. But it wouldn't be a good thing for me to marry a normal girl, with whom I couldn't properly share a survivor's feelings. Enduring weeks and weeks with a wound festering with wriggling insects is unimaginable for anyone who hasn't lived through it. It's simply unacceptable. One can be helped and comforted, but being understood—that's something else entirely.

"My scar is too noticeable. It stripes my head, it's eye-catching. I'd like to hide it; it messes me up. Even with a big herdsman's hat, I can't cover it. If my memory forgets a thing, some people say, 'Yes, he lost his mind, you can see that.' If I screw up, they tell me, 'Don't worry, my friend, it isn't you, it's that bad wound showing on your head.' Some folks may even whisper about me, 'No point in asking him what tribe he's from: it's drawn on his skull.' I think it's humiliating to be marked this way. You can be mocked anytime, you can be insulted when you meet up with the children of killers. I think it influences my distrust of girls, since they can talk "hush-hush" about my wound. I'd rather stand aside, so it won't be noticed. I like to walk; I'm never tired; I have fun striding along the road, crossing prairies, going up into forests, looking down from hilltops. I love looking at the land; maybe I'd enjoy traveling.

"There are survivors who want to forget a little, since they have stayed the way they're supposed to be. They don't forget anything, but they shorten their memories so they can look toward the future. They don't want to wind their lives around their memories. Or they fear bothering and boring people by always telling what happened; they feel in the way, they're afraid of ending up unwanted, so they try to keep quiet. They feel they've lost enough already. Or they're terrified of the authorities and dread going against the new rules about correct behavior. They listen politely to the humanitarian advice. They learn the proper manners for mutual understanding to avoid any reprisals. They hope for advantages and decide to adopt the politics of national reconciliation.

"But someone who's badly wounded just couldn't care less. He ignores manners, disdains all that hugging. He doesn't want to have anything to do with Hutus, refuses to watch those guilty people rejoining their families, weighing the bags of their harvests, piling up goods. The first thing he sees in his new existence is his scar, and he thinks about the consequences that secretly come with it. He knows he must live with it all on his own.

Wherever he looks, he finds the genocide, simply from guessing that everyone's eyes all around are on his survivor's scar.

"Obviously he talks about it. He snatches up all the good reasons to keep talking about it. And he always tells the same story, like me. He'll never tire of that tale. Happiness . . . would be a quiet mind. It would be to slip freely past all troubles and sorrows, but when I look around me, those are all I see."

A STARRY SKY

Telling survivors: "You also interest us when you go on living." Stopping for a moment, meeting people, writing down the stories of those who try to leave the past behind, of those who race or flee on ahead, of those who are overtaken by anguish. Reporting on people's fears, leaving room for the doubt and indecision that can arise. Noting how people speak in public, how they "tell" themselves differently on each of my visits; paying attention to their ways of remembering, and of imagining their memories . . .

With nightfall come a sudden, gentle coolness, and silence. And the dust of the day finally settles. I sit on the doorstep of Marie-Louise Kagoyire's house, a Primus close at hand, and watch the guards take up their posts at the service station across the street.

Drowsing all day, half lying in doorways or in the shade of an open corrugated-metal shed, their hats tipped over their faces, the guards come awake like owls in the darkness to watch over a warehouse, a humanitarian organization center, or sometimes simply a brand-new van. Dressed in rags like herd boys, holding long staves, sparing of words, they are often old men without any family, solitary widowers, sometimes feebleminded or pretending to be, traumatized souls for whom this job means a daily meal.

Occasionally they come from far away, like the guard at the Kébissi *cabaret*. After the massacre of his wife and their nine children, he fled Bisesero, a village in the Kibuye area that became a trouble spot during Operation Turquoise and figures in polemics about the French army's role in the genocide.[*] This silent man quietly comes to begin his surveillance, taking his place at the end of the *cabaret*'s veranda. He never touches a bottle, takes no part in the conversations, and stares out into the night, sometimes mumbling vaguely comprehensible tirades that seem to concern "out there."

From the veranda of the Kébissi, you can see Nyamata with its tiny fires and, beyond them, hills tinged with pink in the dying sunlight, backed by their shadows. It's a lovely spot for confronting the vague melancholy of twilight, with a slight buzz from one's first beers and the fatigues of a hot day. One after the other, regular customers emerge from the darkness, heading home from the office, or dropping in for their after-dinner visit, or coming up the hill from another *cabaret* lower down, all with many hearty greetings. The Kébissi (formerly the Kayumba Bizness Center), much favored by a group of neighborhood intellectuals, occupies a place of honor on the heights of Kayumba. Mama Mwungera runs the grocery counter and her daughter Mukamana serves drinks on the veranda, where the first arrivals sit sprawled on couches while others take the stools, their bottles within easy reach on a low table. There they joke around, gossip, have a good laugh, and—more than anywhere else—talk late into the night, setting the world completely to rights, especially the one that's not right under their noses.

---

[*] *French troops initiated and completed Operation Turquoise in June–August 1994; it was said to be a humanitarian mission, but it principally protected the exodus of Hutus to Congo. Rwanda has long accused France of having trained the militias that slaughtered minority Tutsis and politically moderate Hutus. —Translator's note*

. . .

. . . Admitting my obsession with the history of this genocide and, inevitably, other genocides. Recognizing the attraction of this extraordinary event, the feeling of bewilderment, vertigo, intoxication. Acknowledging the excitement of driving all over the hills. Evoking the disgust, the loathsome impressions that become unshakable, mixed in with the feeling of experiencing close-up, in a way you hadn't thought possible, a calamity of history previously addressed only in books, films, and newspapers, a calamity that upsets, then realigns, a journalist's trajectory. Observing the changes wrought by time as it phases out the turmoil in survivors' lives and seems so beneficial to almost everyone but is horrendously more helpful to the killers, changes that diminish neither the hatred nor the anguish but only mask them a little . . .

Marie-Louise now lives at one end of the town's main street. This house, which she designed down to the smallest details, is not like the various places she owns in Nyamata and once lived in. Before the genocide, she and her husband, Léonard, the leading local businessman, lived at the other end of the street in a splendid home surrounded by outbuildings and a garden. After the killings, her harrowing ordeal in Burundi, and her eventual return to Rwanda, Marie-Louise rented her old home to a humanitarian organization and moved to another spacious house with lots of flowers, but she found it too isolated. There are no trees or gardens around her newest home, no sheds or chicken coops, only narrow buildings that shelter the place: a series of small rooms for her orphans, her friends, her guests, and the office with her computer setup.

Widowed, physically weakened by her difficult escape, Marie-Louise calmly went about getting back to business in a devastated Nyamata. She had her fields cleared, and her shop quickly became the liveliest *cabaret* in town; but this plump and refined lady's glory days are behind her, for, as she explains, "I had a door put on this little shop; the trade came back, but the hope was gone. Léonard and I, we went from one project to the next, our plans did well, we were loved and respected. Now I see all life with a somber eye, watching out everywhere for dangers large and small. I have lost the one who loved me . . ." And so she decided to delegate responsibility, abandon the fields, break up the herds, sell her jewelry, and withdraw to her new house to struggle against sadness with the people she loves, especially the orphans she has taken in, plus Engelbert and Jean-Baptiste, her strong right arm, and of course the computer, her new passion.

Marie-Louise's curiosity and eclecticism are just amazing. With only a primary-school education, a hesitant command of French, and experience limited strictly to commerce, she launched herself overnight into the world of computers: learning French and computerese, familiarizing herself with various softwares, desktop publishing, Internet linkups. She opened the first cybercafé in Nyamata, added a satellite dish, a flat-screen TV, the newspaper *Le Monde*'s collection of DVD films and other classic masterpieces, and turned her house into a temple for movie buffs.

Only her cook, Janvière, and the exquisite fare of her table recall her former life of gracious elegance. People know this, and farm women stop at her gate to offer a lamb or a sack of particularly fine bananas before going on to the market, while discriminating gourmets just happen to pass by at lunchtime. Marie-Louise's ambition from now on is to make a success of her new life as a survivor. Everything seems simple with her: her sorrow, her anguish, her hatred. And that's why it's so pleasant to buy her a Coke and spend an evening chatting about this and that and everything else—sometimes with Engelbert there, too, before he gets too drunk and aggressive.

Like many of Marie-Louise's companions, Engelbert organizes his wanderings with care, and if he hasn't returned by nightfall, it's because he's in a dive on the same street as the clinic, nursing a bottle in one of those crummy *cabarets* with dirty green walls and flickering candles, where *urwagwa* rejected earlier that day because of its ongoing yellowish fermentation is consumed by a less fastidious clientele.

Farther along that deserted street, muffled shouting marks the Anfield Room, a den with barred windows where the other large color screen in the area rebroadcasts English and Spanish championship soccer matches every evening. In a furnace of tropical sweat, fans crammed bare-chested and sweltering on benches cheer and argue about the prowess of African stars playing on prestigious teams, players like Makélélé, Eto'o, Essien, Drogba, whose jerseys, purchased secondhand, outshine those of Beckham, Ronaldo, or Zidane. On the local playing field, at the end of the street, lynx-eyed fans—especially the little ones—who can't afford a ticket to the Anfield Room wear themselves out kicking around the soccer ball abandoned at last by the older youths.

At the central intersection of Nyamata, where the clinic street crosses the main thoroughfare, looms Chicago's warehouse. More than Marie-Louise or Théoneste, his neighbor, the beer wholesaler Chicago is living proof of a kind of commercial atavism. A wealthy businessman in Gikongoro who escaped the massacres, he returned from exile in Burundi and landed in Nyamata sick, starving, and broke. With a borrowed pittance and a backfiring jalopy, he started a business, and a few years later his belly is the roundest, his wife the most stylish, and his truck the sturdiest for a hundred kilometers around. Late into the night, bicyclists appear at his warehouse, balance cases of Primus on their luggage racks, and set off to restock restaurants and *cabarets*.

But Chicago never forgets. On the porch of his warehouse are chairs where his friends, often down on their luck, come to sit and find bottles of beer slipped miraculously into their hands. Tite, the soccer wonder of the 1960s; Dominique, one of the Kayumba Forest band; Jean, a former judge; and other townspeople who like to chew the fat in this strategically situated spot. Tonight they are tasting, with much commentary, the latest Amstel, a red ale that Chicago has brought back from Bujumbura. Out in the marketplace flicker the charcoal fires around which shadowy figures watch, serving late customers before stretching out on their *pagnes* until the market reopens in the morning. In the distance, illuminated by neon lights framing the windows of hairdressing salons, groups of young people listen to rattling Nigerian juju music or the latest percussive *coupé-décalé* hits from the Ivory Coast.

From oral to written, the transition is not only from what is spoken to what is written down, but from what is put into words for *others* to what is put into words for *oneself*. There were always at least two of us talking in Nyamata, Kibungo, or Rilima; in Paris, only one person is writing down what was said back in Africa. At the moment of writing at a desk, the person who spoke in Nyamata inevitably gives way to the sentences now being written. The author works on his words, reworks them, and must of necessity deflect them from their original destination in the act of transcribing them for readers. The words—intact and authentic—change their meaning ever so slightly as he lines them up on paper. Directing and editing the *giving of evidence* for a book means transforming the witnesses into characters in a book.

What is *inexpressible* about genocide is not the horror, the abomination. Why would it be? What is *beyond words* is the destruction of memory along with the destruction of human beings. It's the destruction of the memories of millions of Jews in Europe or Tutsis in Rwanda, because only they could have spoken of that destruction of their memories—only they, who were destroyed. In Nyamata, most survivors believe they should speak for the dead, but also believe they simply can't, not even in love or friendship, not even on behalf of a relative or neighbor killed beside them in the papyrus swamps. They try anyway, because they feel they will not be believed without the support of those who died. Writing can't replace this testimony of the dead but helps to bring it into the survivors' stories somehow. Writing can also retrace what isn't said.

How do you write down the living words of others? I never really came to terms with this question until I discovered how deeply it preoccupied the readers of my book about the genocide's survivors, *Life Laid Bare*. How does one trim, choose, edit, construct a text from oral testimony? It isn't easy, it can be quite complicated, but it's a self-evident form of writing when the motivation is essentially literary, and when one is moved by the desire to bring the reader into the genocidal universe and to pass along a story, so that the book will eventually lead its own existence and its characters live out their destinies, like the real or fictional people in all books, and so that what was said will make its way from author to reader. The story, the people, the interviews, the words and images, come together in a text that translates what happened in a different way. This kind of literature is comparatively sinuous, slow, belated, metaphorical, inspired, but quite effective for transmitting information from one point to another when the direct path, the straight path, the one journalists are the first to use, is blocked. And that path is systematically blocked after a genocide—whether in Europe, Turkey, or Rwanda—because journalists are stymied, and their readers and viewers just as much so, if not more, by such a stupefying event.

What do the people in Nyamata think about this? It's impossible to answer for them, but they surely think more kindly than ill of what I am doing; otherwise I could not have written this book after the other two.

Life Laid Bare took shape in an atmosphere heavy with distrust. A white Frenchman spending whole days running around the hills questioning the same people, mostly farm women—that could only be suspicious. But luck and felicitous encounters earned me the benefit of the doubt; then publication of the book reassured everyone. Not only had the Frenchman repaid their trust, but people admitted they had learned a lot about the genocide from reading the book—even those who had contributed to it, because they read and recognized in their own narratives ideas or impressions, often muddled, that they had previously kept secret or implicit, since they concerned things too painful and perhaps too confusing or incredible for other people to grasp.

Thanks to that revelation, the idea for *Machete Season* could be considered—in a climate of utter incomprehension, of course, because going every morning for months to talk with genocidal killers in a penitentiary was beyond all understanding for the survivors, for the authorities, and for the families and friends of the killers. No one, over the course of my many visits to the prison in Rilima, ever asked me what I expected or obtained from my trips or showed the slightest curiosity about what the killers might have to say. When the book was published, almost everyone ignored what the killers in fact had said to me, and focused instead on the texts I wrote to introduce the testimonial chapters, especially the one in which I tried to deal with history and the analogies between the Jewish and Tutsi genocides.

As for the killers, they never dipped into the first book, of course, and hardly glanced at the second one. They received the latter—an unexpected, glossy white object—and said thank you as they would have for any other gift from abroad, without the slightest remark. When they were released, no one in Rwanda—neither the government nor the judges—challenged them over their quoted remarks in the book, even though these radically contradicted the testimony they'd given during their trials. Realizing that the book wasn't doing them any immediate harm, they denied nothing of what they had freely told me when they'd believed themselves imprisoned for life.

This would be a good moment to take another look at the astonishing loquacity of the killers (especially Léopord's willingness to confess), a talkativeness so unlike the silences, lies, denials, and forgetfulness that seem to be de rigueur among all killers in other genocides, as I have observed. Why did *these* men—unlike their Hutu, German, Turkish, or Khmer counterparts—agree to remember and to talk? Were they revealing extraordinary personalities? Certainly not, but their state of mind reflects the exceptional circumstances in which, as the months went by, they began to speak.

When I first met them in Rilima, they were incarcerated among seven thousand other detainees, unaware that they would eventually be released much sooner than anticipated, and, given the high mortality rate in the penitentiary, they believed themselves imprisoned for life. Since they had already been convicted, they did not feel their accounts could either help or hurt them, particularly as they were convinced I wouldn't tell a soul what they said—not the judges, or the neighbors, or their families—except in some old book published unimaginably far away.

Moreover, when they did agree to speak, they hadn't yet

either returned to the marshes or had to confront the accusing eyes of a foreigner or a victim's family. So they were living in a kind of bubble in Rilima, where lies and silence no longer served a purpose. And while they knew I abhorred their actions and could never be persuaded to feel sympathy for them, they eventually realized that my objective was not to accuse them.

Paradoxically, they are still willing to talk with me after their release, as if carried along by their own momentum, so to speak. They remain cordial and accessible, never making the slightest allusion to the earlier book I wrote about them. Our interviews take place in each man's home without anyone there except my translator, Innocent, a familiar presence, and whenever someone else appears—even a prison buddy or one of the killing gang— the men retract their words or fall silent.

The killers were not a monolithic group. At every stage of my work on *Machete Season* and on this present book, each of the men reacted differently. Ignace, at first the most cunning and hardheaded of the bunch, became at the end the one most interested in my project and most precise in his accounts. Pio was just the opposite: quite attentive in the penitentiary garden, he turned into an outrageous liar during our last interviews. Is this because Ignace—older, poorer—is more disillusioned and aware of their collective failure? Have marriage, inheriting a banana patch, and once again enjoying soccer games given Pio a new lease on life? I don't know and I haven't paid any attention to the men's moods and motives. I simply listen to them and take them as they come.

My relationships with the survivors whom I wrote about in *Life Laid Bare* are sincere, and much more complicated and unpredictable than those I have with the killers. In his or her own way, each survivor became involved in the preparation of that book; all of them read it—or at least the sections containing their accounts—and made that clear to me. Since its publication they've been questioned about the book by friends, by relatives, by colleagues, and often by foreigners.

Without giving any explanation, some of these survivors—like Édith, a friend, or Odette, who does not open up easily—did not want to pursue the adventure when I returned to Nyamata. As for the others, Sylvie changes attitudes the way she changes outfits: one day she is emphatic, attentive, and pessimistic; the next day elusive or absent; yet another day frivolous, with an optimism bordering on fantasy. She likes provocation, not for the pleasure of originality or contradiction, but to avoid getting stuck in a role and to emphasize the complexity of her moods. She is the opposite of Francine, who approaches each interview as if it were the latest installment of a serial, a story she's trying to tell without leaving out a single detail. For others, the first book changed the way they deal with the tape recorder: for example, the moment the machine clicks on, Marie-Louise's chatter turns unexpectedly wooden, and when I mention this to her, she bursts out laughing. Innocent now enjoys taking extra trouble over his answers and helping to produce a book; Jean-Baptiste Munyankore finds increased intellectual gratification in thinking not only about what he says but about his character as a witness, and he insists on wearing his Sunday suit and having a Primus before beginning each interview.

The strangest participant, at least during these past few years, has been Berthe. In a way she is also the loneliest, in spite of the sisters and children who now fill her life, and the most melancholy. She speaks in a soft, low voice. It seems she takes pleasure in talking about herself, which she does with increasing precision—not as a form of therapy, but in recognition of who she is and who she might have been. She lost her parents and her many siblings in Ntamara and in the marshes; since then her hopes to be a nurse have faded in the face of an obligation to farm. She is a wonderful, formidable young woman worthy of what should have been a fascinating life.

Jeannette, Janvier, Angélique, and Claudine behave with the same unaffected openness as they did before: Jeannette with her same naïveté, always overwhelmed by what's happening to her; Janvier prudent as ever, especially now that, unable to reconstitute the family's cattle herd, he has joined the army; Angélique always clearheaded and articulate; Claudine displaying now and again her gift for tart derision.

Still and all, the years do pass; affection and friendship take root among us. In addition, the survivors are picking up the official language about the genocide that they hear on the radio, in church, at the gaçaças—as are the Hutus, who now glibly throw around words like *survivors* and *genocide* that they once found impossible to use. And the survivors no longer wonder at the historical interest aroused by the Tutsi genocide, nor do they become quite so emotional over my questions and the ensuing painful memories, having apparently grown accustomed to this dialogue, thanks in part to other interviews some of them have given since the publication of the earlier books.

At night, the stars come so close to Nyamata that they no longer form a vault but create an array of sparkling fires: sometimes blinking, sometimes dazzling, almost hot, as they are in the desert. No matter what shape the moon is in, when wind has swept away the clouds, those stars illuminate this town without streetlights and the country roads abandoned by vehicles as if it were inconceivable to leave these hills in darkness. It's child's play to find the Big Dipper and other well-known constellations, despite the distraction of shooting stars that flare up in a distant blaze or track thick streaks across the sky, crisscrossing without ever colliding. It's an endless treat to watch their celestial frolics. Yet, no one ever seems to enjoy the show around here—neither the grown-ups gossiping in their front yards, nor the little rascals plotting behind the bushes, nor the passersby staggering tipsily through the streets or heading soberly on home.

All night long, forms pass in front of Marie-Louise's place, whispering in the semidarkness. Cows low softly in chorus, heads nodding, sated or exhausted by their day of grazing. Birdcalls give way to the yipping of stray dogs in the distance, barking alone or in packs, answered by the plaintive howl of a gray jackal like the ones often encountered along a path.

GOD NEVER LEFT

Late on a pleasant afternoon, Lisa Rosenthal served tea on the lawn in front of her house in Kfar Blum, a kibbutz way up in the north of Israel, a warm and verdant region bordered by Lebanon and the Golan Heights. Across from us, an enthusiastic audience was watching a hotly contested volleyball match, while off to the side teenagers lounging in deck chairs flirted and sipped milk shakes.

Everyone addressed Lisa Rosenthal affectionately by her first name on this kibbutz, where she has lived ever since her arrival in 1963—the year, she recalled, of the big flood. Born in Prague, deported at the age of eighteen to the extermination camp at Birkenau, she had survived. A tall, elegant, and erudite lady, fluent in five languages, a whimsical person in the image of the old Mitteleuropean intelligentsia (it's now impossible to imagine just how much that caste will be missed), she told me about her odyssey: her family and studies, the roundup of the Jews, the exodus, and now gardening with her friend and compatriot, Irina. She spoke as well of her long solitude, in spite of the warm respect she enjoyed among the kibbutzniks.

At one point she said, "I no longer feel Czechoslovakian, and I don't feel Israeli, way off in this kibbutz. I don't feel Jewish anymore, of course. Frankly, I feel a little lonely."

"You don't feel Jewish anymore, 'of course'? What does that mean?"

"I mean, not Jewish anymore the way I was with my family: prayers in the Maisel Synagogue, the poppy-seed strudels, the marriages and celebrations of Yom Kippur or Purim at the Shalom Restaurant in my neighborhood of Josephov, the Jewish quarter. When I left Birkenau, the very idea of God seemed utterly grotesque to me. And reading the Torah—of no interest. My Judaism, like all the rest, had gone down the drain with the bathwater."

Twenty years later, doubtless because of the sorrowful irony in her voice, I can still hear how she described the idea of a faith destroyed in the camps along with everything else.

Many, many other survivors of the Shoah have said the same thing, all in their own ways. In a conversation with his compatriot, the writer Fernando Cameron, Primo Levi said, "Since there was Auschwitz, God cannot exist. Auschwitz is the proof of the nonexistence of God. The dilemma. I don't find. I look. It's important that the second action comes second."

Like most Rwandans, Innocent Rwililiza knows the biblical history of the Jewish people but nothing about them in modern times, and when I questioned him about Levi's words, he reread them carefully before answering.

"On the one hand, saying that makes sense, naturally. The dilemma—it's harsh. And we, too, grapple with it. Up on Kayumba we called to God from morning till night, and I finally tired of seeing nothing arrive but machetes. And like many others, I, too, wondered about that question—the life of God—when the killings began and we still believed in something, and again at the end, when we no longer had faith in anything. Because during the killings, we simply didn't think anymore about believing.

"On the other hand, God is someone we can't ignore, we can't dishonor—not here, in any case. God . . . we Blacks have even stronger belief than you Whites do. That Italian philosopher did have the right to suggest his nonexistence, but he cannot get a hearing in Africa."

In Africa, atheism seems incomprehensible. The idea of a world without God, whatever God's influence might be, appears inconceivable, and the killings haven't changed that one bit: thirteen years later, it's impossible to find a single person in the Nyamata area who admits out loud to becoming an atheist because of the genocide.

At the time, however, as Innocent makes clear, that calamity had truly exhausted the faith of many people and still bedevils it today, in the way Cassius sees religion, for example: "Perhaps God could not fight against all those evildoers. I still believe in him, because otherwise it would be too risky. But he is no longer our every chance, and I don't count on him at all the way I used to."

On the morning of April 11, 1994, when the massacres began at the marketplace and three immaculate white armored vehicles from UNAMIR (the UN Assistance Mission in Rwanda) came to rescue the white priests and nuns at the church parish complex, the first reflex of the Tutsi faithful was in stark contrast to that of the Hutus. The Tutsis turned immediately toward God, hurrying to seek refuge within the churches of Nyamata and Ntarama. Those who could not get there fled into the forests or down to the marshes, where the fugitives formed groups to pray and sing, until the first hunting expeditions appeared. Meanwhile the Hutus abandoned both Catholic and Protestant churches, except for the ones sheltering Tutsis, where they went in for the kill.

Adalbert Munzigura remembered the last time he was in the Kibungo church: "On Sunday morning we appeared at the appointed hour for Mass; the Tutsis did not come. They had already fled into the bush in fear of reprisals, driving their goats and cows before them. That disappointed us greatly, especially on a Sunday. Anger hustled us outside the church door. We left the Lord and our prayers inside to rush home. We changed from our Sunday best into our workaday clothes, we grabbed clubs and machetes, we went straight off to killing. In the marshes I was appointed killing boss . . . In prison I was appointed charismatic leader, because I sang intensely. I enjoyed the hallelujahs."

Alphonse remembered the second day of the genocide: "The Thursday when we went to the church in Ntarama, the people just lay there in the dim light, the wounded visible between the pews, the unhurt hiding beneath the pews, and the dead in the aisles all the way to the foot of the altar. We were the only ones making a commotion. Them, they were waiting for death in the calm of the church. For us, being in a house of God was no longer of any importance . . ."

Alphonse's wife, Consolée Murekatete, experienced the situation quite differently: "Oh, I was afraid. I was obsessed by a divine malediction: I could see clearly that those unnatural killings would call down a punishment from heaven. All that blood would lead to damnation. I knew that God could intervene at any moment, as in the Bible. I thought of Egypt, of Gomorrah and the like. The day we left the house empty-handed on the way to Congo, in the sound of bullets, our flight seemed a calamity worse than death. We were losing our wealth, our goods, abandoning our ancestral fields; we were leaving a roof and a parish to go off to endless nights of perdition on the roads, in tumult and raging sickness. I thought, Here the time of vengeance is come, with the apocalypse and its darkness."

Although the Hutus walked away from God, they didn't go so far as to break with him. Common sense drove them to stay in contact, in secret, because a little more cheating wouldn't make any difference, as Fulgence explained: "I was a deacon, the one on the hill of Kibungo who made arrangements for Christian gatherings . . . During the killings, I chose not to pray to God. We had removed the Tutsis from God's work, from the creation of mankind and even of animals. I sensed that it was not appropriate to involve Him in that . . . Still, when dread would grip me suddenly in the night, if I had done too much during the day, I would ask God as a personal favor to let me stop for just a few days."

Ignace confirmed this: "For a little while, we were no longer ordinary Christians, we had to forget our duties learned in cate-chism class. We had first of all to obey our leaders—and God only afterward, very long afterward, to make confession and penance. When the job was done."

Only Léopord, a man given to extremes, affirmed that the renunciation was complete: "Some claim today that they sent up prayers during the killings to gain God's forgiveness. They are shamming. When they sang hallelujah, it was in contentment for having unearthed a Tutsi. No one ever even heard an Ave Maria or the like: they're only trying to jump in front of their colleagues in line for repentance. In truth, we thought that from then on we could manage for ourselves without God. The proof: we killed even on Sunday without ever noticing it."

Like other small African towns, Nyamata has no bookstores (Kigali has only two). For many Africans, schoolbooks and the Bible are their only reading. Strangely enough, it's the Old Testa-ment that is, if not the one the most quoted by the priests, at least the most influential of the two, and the one most read by the faithful, who when they pray address themselves essentially to

Yahweh, the all-powerful Lord, menacing and intransigent. They are much more familiar with his fury or complicity with Abraham, Moses, or Solomon than they are with Jesus or the Virgin Mary, who aren't as popular.

This special relationship with a vengeful God complicates our understanding of the accounts of renunciations, doubts, or spiritual failings that may have assailed the fugitives in the marshes, because, as the survivor Jean-Baptiste Munyankore points out, "In the marshes, some were murmuring that God no longer existed, since He hadn't sent us the slightest sign. But no one stood up to challenge Him out loud, because they had known Him as too dominating, and because in spite of everything, it was too risky."

Berthe, Claudine, and Angélique, adolescents or young women at the time of the massacres, are the survivors who best express their spiritual distress:

Angélique: "I wasn't a very conscientious baptized child. I followed along and recited without begging for anything. Still, during the first days of the genocide, I became quite observant, really: I prayed every day, I communed nonstop, but not like before. When we had to spend a whole day in our watery hiding places, we prayed to forget the frightening suffering of machete blows, but deep down, we weren't praying anymore to be saved. The more corpses we saw among the reeds, the less we believed in God, especially since we'd begged so much for His helping hand.

"We no longer hoped, but we went on praying. We prayed so as to keep ourselves a little company, so as not to get discouraged from hiding for so long, alone in the mud. And because we couldn't find any other words to say anymore except the ones in prayers. Finally we stopped praying. We didn't think about believing or not believing after that, because in any case we no longer thought at all. There was nothing left worth saying."

Claudine: "After the liberation, time recalled us to our duties as Christians. Myself, I had lost my whole family without any trace of their deaths. One day when it hadn't rained for a long time, while I was out in a field, fatigue and sorrow overwhelmed me. Loneliness held me so tight that I found myself praying to find at least one relative again. A few days later I spotted one of my older brothers on the road: he was alive, and I hadn't known this. That's how I started being Christian again.

"But it took five years before I began once more to feel anguish about the hereafter, because during all those years, I felt the killings could start up afresh, so I feared only the machete. I had to wait until I'd calmed down and believed in the safety of my hill, and had met my husband, a very pious man. You must feel at peace to understand the return of the religious dread of death.

"I became a Pentecostalist like my husband. The atmosphere is not pleasant anymore. I hear Hutus singing that God has forgiven. I know the farmer who cut down one of my sisters; he was released from Rilima for free, without having apologized. His face is still evil. In the *cabaret* he boasts about fearing neither God nor man nor returning to prison. When we meet on the road, we shake hands. I accept, so that God will not think badly of me, so His wrath will not fall upon my family. I fear His reproaches more than the scolding of the authorities. Personally, I pray only with an eye to the afterlife, to keep a better fate in store for my family after death. As for life on earth, I place no hope at all in divine intervention."

Berthe: "I was a child who prayed every Sunday; I'd gone through all the ceremonies and baptisms and suchlike. In the marshes I began to pray to be spared. We used to pray in the mornings before burying ourselves in the papyrus. Some old mamas liked to pray a double shift in the evening, and they recited litanies with rosaries. The longer the killings lasted, the more discouraged we got about praying. During their hunting expeditions, the *interahamwe* would sing that God had abandoned the Tutsis or that He'd left Rwanda and wouldn't be back until after the final massacre, and we—we began to believe them.

"The day of the great massacre of April 30, I lost too much heart; I stopped praying. First I believed Satan was stronger than God, the direct opposite of what I'd been taught. Afterward I really didn't give a spit about God or Satan: I had no more doubts or certainties, I had nothing left to believe except that I was going to be cut. There was no one to help me anymore, nothing for me to think except how to last another day with the children I was looking after.

"Time pushed us out of the marshes alive. Life drew us on, and the fear of God came back to us naturally. I thought that since I'd survived, I really ought to become a believer again, that I had endured enough of the Hutus' wickedness to be spared God's anger, which can be terrible indeed. But I don't go to Sunday Mass anymore. That church door, it makes you recoil, if you remember the killers inside swinging machetes—and if you hear them now! Quivering and singing their heads off in choirs to unload their sins, without a word about what they did.

"I think you cannot share prayers that set no truth free. To my mind, the survivors go to church to be with others like them and feel less lonely. The killers go there to show they're smiling and behaving properly with people. And the authorities in Kigali have heavily mobilized the church in their politics of reconciliation. Because in a church, you're expected to swallow whatever the priest says. You accept what you don't believe in when you happen to be sitting between two of the faithful in a holy place. Once outside, though—goodbye.

"Before, religion anchored education. Rwandan schoolchildren were enthusiastic and the priests strutted around, highly respected. Now we know that the people butchered in the church had been gathered there by the priest. For three days he kept telling them to keep calm and pray. And then one morning he left the church in a white vehicle without a word of farewell to his flock, not even 'Good luck.' Before, you inherited your religion from your parents, and if you were baptized Catholic, you were buried Catholic. Today it's a whole back-and-forth. The faithful spend six months with the Adventists, and if they don't feel satisfied, they swing over to the Pentecostalists, and if that still doesn't do it, they try out the Dominicans. Some old mamas switch three times a year.

"Many of the once faithful have quit, like me; many whip up their enthusiasm in new churches. On our hill, five churches have popped up in five years."

And many more in Nyamata. When Marie-Louise built her lovely brick house at the entrance to the town, she was seeking serenity. So one Sunday she is aghast to hear, on the other side of her wall, the thundering din of a powerfully amplified Mass. The Temple of Zion, a sect born in the posh neighborhoods of Kigali, has just set up shop next door—with a show-off preacher who proclaims himself the thirteenth apostle and harangues frenzied choirs, delirious musical combos, and hysterical flocks, unleashing veritable howls during sessions of tears and lamentations.

Doctors and nurses from the hospital troop through, along with prosperous merchants' wives, soccer coaches, pretty women, lots of young people, and plenty of Hutus. On the main street, Restoration's Church competes with Jehovah's Witnesses and, farther away on the hill of Mayange, the Temperance Church.

And so it goes from sect to sect, through bush and hamlet all the way to the Rilima penitentiary, as Joseph-Désiré Bitero confirms from death row:

"It's truly God who is not abandoning us. He alone helps us to thwart the troubles reaching out for us here below. Reason why prisoners are the most fervent in prayer. On death row, we hope to live as long as possible. We try never to feel alone. Only through the grace of God can one live in the penitentiary without being killed. Here, churches and sects take turns all day long. The prisoners are influenced by the most promising sermons, so there can be startling shifts in religious loyalty. Many sects distribute provisions and good-quality clothing, advertise themselves seductively, forecast forgiveness and more, and are lavish with absolutions. They are on parade."

When at the top of his form, the Temple of Zion preacher—in tight pants and a ruffled shirt—adores performing exorcisms. One day he calls on those suffering from AIDS to step forward; another day, he calls up cripples. He touches them, shouting to the heavens, "Cast out the demons of AIDS!" and "Begone, ye demons of paralysis!" He revs up the choirs, draws hallelujahs from the crowd, leaps up and dances around until it's time to announce that the faithful will be completely cured. One day he promises marriage partners to survivors who lost their husbands; another time he yells out, "Let the demons of genocide be driven hence!"—and calls the killers to step forward, promising them a ticket to paradise.

Marie-Louise is staggered by what's happening next door. "I don't believe people are going there entirely sincerely. I think they're getting together to lose themselves in the excitement. The atmosphere is heady, the music joyful, lots of young people show up. They appreciate the shortcuts: you don't have to learn the Bible, recite long prayers—it's just hallelujahs and suchlike simple penitence. Baptisms take place in a pond they call Jordan, where the water is said to take away all sins and sickness. The killers are the first in line. They hope the congregation will pray for them, help them be forgiven."

This great wave of religious sects is not a new development in Africa, especially in that sub-Saharan zone that is losing its bearings, and these sects provide Sunday spectacles both burlesque and pathetic. Rwanda, once protected by a robust clergy of Flemish allegiance but deserted by a panicked church hierarchy during the genocide, has become as helpless as its neighbors under this onslaught.

When he has four or five Primuses under his belt, Innocent Rwililiza often falls prey to painful memories of his first wife and their son, murdered in the church in Nyamata, and then he speaks with unusual bluntness: "During those first days up on Kayumba, there was a boy who ran from the hunters carrying a radio and some batteries. In the evenings we'd listen, hoping to hear some pope or at any rate a bishop forbid the Hutus to cut children, at least in the churches. But that little Polish pope, he kept his mouth shut, except afterward, to defend his bishop Misago when he was caught with Tutsi bloodstains on his chasuble. The Most Reverend Misago was the smartest of my instructors at the teachers' academy, a remarkable pedagogue, quite pleasant, very patient, a learned man who studied the Gospels in Rome, and he was up to his neck in the massacres in Gikongoro."[*]

---

[*] *Bishop Augustin Misago of Gikongoro, the highest-ranking clergyman to have been arrested for involvement in the 1994 killings, has been identified by two human rights organizations, African Rights and Human Rights Watch, as a genocidal criminal. In April 1999 he was charged with helping organize massacres with local government and security officials, turning away those who came to him for help, and actively participating in the killings, including the massacre of ninety Tutsi children in the Marie Merci School. Bishop Misago claimed that the Kagame regime was persecuting prominent Hutus, and then the Vatican accused the Rwandan government of attacking the Church. Despite the testimony of many survivors from Gikongoro, in June 2000 the judge at his trial in Kigali dismissed all charges against him as hearsay. —Translator's note*

Marie-Louise is less bitter, more resigned to disillusionment: "Christians did not behave with much humanity during the genocide. I am not disappointed with God and I keep my rosary for Him, but I no longer feel comfortable in the Christian fold. I don't go to Mass anymore. I used to love Mass, and the singing warmed my heart. I found joy in the baptisms and weddings. Now I go and wait for the ceremony to be over. I've stopped feeling cheered and convivial at such affairs. The church has become a theater. Survivors go there to give thanks for still being alive. Killers walk humbly to the altar to receive the Eucharist. If they've murdered ten or fifteen people, they swallow three wafers, but still without a word of apology for those they killed."

Other killers don't waste time like that anymore, and they're frank about why, like Ignace: "Whoever goes to church hopes to take away some benefit from it. You beg for rain, full harvests, more children, good health, cordial relations. It's useless to take Communion for killings that can draw resentful attention to you and get you into trouble. Praying for what's past, that's just pointless. On Sundays I would rather look for a bit of good fortune in my own fields than wear out a nice suit of clothes."

On the veranda of a *cabaret* up in Nyarunazi, a bottle of banana beer in hand, Boniface comments on the above remarks: "I can't agree with him, but I quite understand what he says. Because I, too, have come back from the dead. I am a priest and a survivor."

A skinny man with a kind smile in a face emaciated by suffering, his eyes jaundiced by malaria and alcohol, Boniface has both the Tutsi cattle breeder's staff and wide-brimmed hat, plus the cowherd's torn jacket and grubby pants. His voice is as deep as it is gentle.

"I was a cattleman, a teacher, a churchgoer, and a Tutsi. We farmed peaceably, experiencing no mistrust of Christians. I followed my dear ones into the marshes—not for better or for worse, but for worse and even worse. Every day they exterminated more of us, and still I could not believe that God would accept the destruction of His own Tutsi people. I would call on God's grace to survive one more day.

"Saved from the muddy water at the End of Days, I thought, If God did send me an angel, I will repay Him. I took up the shepherd's staff to go study theology in the diocese. I became a priest assigned to Kibungo, where I preach at the altar. Of course, I must restrain myself: I must bear the sight, in my congregation, of those who hunted us down with machetes.

"In my sermons, I speak of God, of commiseration, of reconciliation. Then things go well with the singing and lessons; the congregation listens attentively. But target the killings, mention the marshes—and the Hutus get angry: their faces scrunch into scowls and that's it. The killings are not acceptable at Mass, or the Hutus take offense. They can stand up during the homily and walk out for good. If I play the killjoy, I empty out my church.

"It's the same thing everywhere: all the priests fear the genocide. So I preach forgiveness, love thy neighbor, help one another during droughts. I persist, I teach patience, because faith has been tarnished. If I personally do not believe that God always redeems Himself in the end, then I saved myself for nothing."

PIO AND JOSIANE

At the end of August 2005, Innocent Rwililiza sent this letter to me in Paris:

> *My dear friend Jean,*
> *Everything is going well here, the weather is quite hot, and soon it will be early September, time to plant beans. Everyone you know is fine and longs to see you again. Without any more chitchat, I'd like to tell you how Pio's wedding turned out.*
> *On Saturday morning, August 13, just after ten o'clock, accompanied by his family, prison friends, and folks from his native province [Gitarama], Pio goes off in a Hilux pickup van to become engaged and give a dowry to Umwrerwa, Josiane (a genocide survivor). Pio's crew is welcomed coldly by the fiancée's invited neighbors and relatives, who are furious about his participation in the killings. The proper words are said, and Pio receives the fiancée in exchange for a cow. There are no openly visible signs of constraint, but the guests grumble to no effect. Pio wears a black suit and black shoes. He is elegant in spite of his somewhat wrinkled face, as you will see in the photo. Josiane wears a splendid white dress rented in Nyamata; she is beautiful, like every fiancée everywhere.*
> *At three o'clock the wedding procession of two vehicles arrives at the church in Nyamata with a noticeable delay that will be slapped*

with a five-thousand-franc fine. Pio is very well attended by a best man whose father is imprisoned in Rilima, under sentence of death for his part in the killings. As for Josiane, she is attended by a sweet girl who, like herself, is a genocide survivor. The situation is the same, very few words on the bride's side but a joyous group around the groom, obviously with some prison colleagues, including Pancrace and the photographer. My wife, Épiphanie, and her daughter Reza are there, attending in place of Rwililiza, Innocent. Pio is very happy about that because he received your little contribution last week, courtesy of Épiphanie, and unlike the other survivors she acts cheerful and doesn't sulk.

After the religious ceremony, the procession drives to Nyarunazi to a reception in Pio's new house, which you have seen. There are enough drinks, even some Primus and a case of Mutzig. Pio lives in a house of adobe and tiles that you have visited; the plastering will be done later because he had to get married in a hurry to counteract the nasty gossip, especially during the gaçaças, that risked preventing his union with Josiane and sending him back to prison.

That is all I could learn about Pio's wedding, thanks to my wife, since I was tied up by an exam that was given this Saturday.

Well, say hello to everyone and until the next time.

Innocent Rwililiza

The first time I heard Pio mention his engagement, we were sitting chatting on felled tree trunks near the construction site of his future house, halfway up the hill between the path and his mother's house on the summit. The site overlooked his banana plantation and, in the distance, offered a panorama of the river winding through the marshes. Pio had just been released after more than seven years in the Rilima penitentiary. He was talking about the dried-out banana plants, the dearth of urwagwa, the aches and stiffness plaguing him in the fields, the pleasure of kicking a soccer ball around with his pals, and the first confrontations with survivors. At one point he said, "I'm building this house to get married. With adobe bricks and fired tiles the way they make them along the Nyabarongo. It's not as good-looking as corrugated metal, but it's cooler and less expensive."

"And the fiancée?"

"She's a good catch. She's from the hill, an acquaintance from primary school. Before the killings, she was still a little girl. When I was released, she had grown up. She has fine dark skin, she's very nice, not too tall or slender. And a very hard worker."

"Your stay in prison didn't interest her?"

"No. We talked about the events of 1994; we didn't dodge around: she said, 'That's how it is, it happened that way, what's the use of going on agonizing over it, life is pulling at us, no one can do anything more about it.' We talked about my life in prison; she said, 'Everyone could have been locked up from one day to the next, and if it wasn't this person, then it was someone else; Providence made the choice, that's not a problem anymore.' Her father was cut in the marshes; she lives with her mama in Gasagara, not far from Alphonse's house. Her mama farms a good-size plot, not rich, not poor. The girl's name is Josiane, she's a Tutsi survivor."

And Pio burst out laughing. A strange laugh, difficult to interpret. Naturally neither I nor Innocent, who was born and taught school on Pio's hill, believed for one second in this marriage between one of the most enterprising killers in the marshes and a girl who had escaped from them. In the weeks that followed, however, we began to wonder, because of the way Pio's mama turned snappish when questioned about it, Pancrace's hilarity whenever *he* was asked, plus the faces some people made and the rumors others passed around in the *cabarets* of Kibungo. And then the banns were posted.

So: what to make of this marriage? The first miracle of recon-ciliation? That's impossible to imagine, in the face of the fierce or stricken expressions occasioned in the two camps by any mention of the affair, if the town commentary swirling around the idyll is to be believed. The triumph of youth, the power of love? A Shakespearean passion? Nothing is less certain, because although Josiane has shown a boldness and tenacity worthy of Juliet, Pio didn't exactly go down into the marshes to play Romeo and avenge his friend Mercutio. He made free play with his machete every day for a good five weeks, searching the papyrus beneath which were hiding, among so many others, Josiane's family.

And yet, the intrigue doubtless came to a head in the marshes. Pio denies it, as does Josiane, who sticks word for word to her husband's account, like everyone else in their group, whenever they do let slip a hint or two on the subject. All of them, that is, except Fifi, the only person to venture an original version of this story—which, although quite precise and probable, does more to deepen the mystery than resolve it.

On weekends Fifi—whose name is Clémentine Mukankusi when she teaches in a local primary school—runs the liveliest *cabaret* in Kibungo. Born here, a Hutu, she's the close friend of the Tutsi president of the Iboka Survivors' Association. She knew Pio and Josiane in her younger days, as their schoolmate. As a girl whose opinion no one wanted during the genocidal weeks of April and May 1994, she watched the flight of her Tutsi friends into the marshes and, every morning, the daily departures of her Hutu friends on their murderous expeditions. Today she admits she couldn't accept a husband from either ethnic group, or choose between the innocent atmosphere of the children's class she teaches at school and the *urwagwa* drinking bouts at her *cabaret*. She is open about her confusion and therefore pays no attention to the quarrels and backbiting on the hills.

So here are the two versions of this marriage, offered in turn by Pio, the husband, and Fifi, the couple's friend—versions that confirm or contradict one another as the episodes unfold, and that harbor an extraordinary mystery.

Pio: "Our acquaintance began in the primary school in Kibungo. Our houses were a few hundred paces apart, and we shared the way to school. On Sundays we went up together to the church in Kibungo to pray. I sang in the choir; Josiane didn't. We were together without any deep friendship because of the age difference."

Fifi: "Pio's family is Hutu, Josiane's is Tutsi; they weren't at all close, exchanging only grim looks. But Pio and Josiane got to like each other in primary school, where they sat every morning on the same bench. It was classroom love, not hot like grownup love. But even though they were little at the time, they maintained a deep intimacy. I was in the same classroom: I couldn't help noticing."

Pio: "During the killings, I believed that Josiane was hiding in the marshes with her family, but I never caught sight of her. Even if I had found her, I wouldn't have dared save her. Sparing someone you knew in the swamp, it was too serious in your comrades' eyes. That could be risky, that could mean more suffering for the acquaintance, whom your colleagues might well cut up slowly to set a good example. Basically, I thought she'd been cut like so many other people. As a school friend, I couldn't be sorry about her anymore, I was too caught up in the hunting expeditions, I was too eager."

Fifi: "According to some who know the young newlyweds well—and I can personally vouch for this because these things are true—Pio uncovered Josiane one morning beneath an armful of papyrus. He stayed his machete. From having been her good friend before, he did not kill her straightaway. He looked all around. Luckily, the few killing colleagues nearby went on with their work without suspicion. Pio managed to hide Josiane in a special place, and to this day only they know where for certain. Myself, I think he took her to a sleeping hut I know of, once used by farm day workers from Ruhengeri. Afterward, Pio continued to go out normally on the expeditions like other young men his age, and in the evenings he could join Josiane in her hideout. He could also make her a woman, of course. In any case, it's there that the preexisting union was reinforced.

"Casual sex in the marshes was a common thing. Lots of Pio's colleagues took a girl from the swamp to use her on dry land in the bushes, before getting on with their hunt. Even several men at a time, if they were hot, even taking her back home if she suited a bachelor's taste. Except that Pio didn't cut her down after using her."

Pio: "When the threatening *inkotanyi* forced us to flee, I led my family away. We passed first through Gitarama, our native prefecture. I knew nothing about Josiane's fate. We believed almost all the Tutsis were dead; I didn't know she was still alive. In the Congo camps, a new life took us over, and it promised to be permanent. Hope of seeing Rwanda again deserted us, so there was no reason for us to think of those back home, living or dead."

Fifi: "When the war turned sour on the killers, Pio went to the hut to warn Josiane about his sad departure. They said their farewells in secret. He hid for two years in Rutobwe, his parents' native commune, near Gitarama.

"The evening of Pio's flight, Josiane left the hut and rejoined the flood of her fellow survivors in Nyamata without a word. It was panic and people everywhere, all filthy rags and misery; no one noticed things anymore amid so much trouble, so no one could be astonished that Josiane was once again among the living. Then she followed her mama to their plot of land, and for two years she waited for news of Pio without knowing if he was alive or dead."

Pio: "Back from Congo, I went up to Nyarunazi, before I was accused and caught. I spent a few weeks in the local jail and later I was taken to the central prison in Rilima. I lasted seven years there. News from the hills did not get through the prison gate. I didn't pay attention to Josiane's memory. The future wasn't offering me any hope of freedom; prison chores occupied my mind. At the time of the trial, I decided to make my confessions, I pleaded guilty like my colleagues, and I wound up pushed toward freedom with the whole gang."

Fifi: "When Pio saw the columns of those former fugitives now heading home from Congo, he followed along, returning with them to Nyarunazi. He was accused of numerous murders and locked up in the penitentiary.

"Josiane was living the survivor's life with her mama on their land. She learned of Pio's imprisonment and was eager to visit him. To get to Rilima, she hid among a small group of Hutu women, thanks to the complicity of a certain Mukandekezi, a neighbor woman very close to Pio. And Josiane visited Pio secretly several times. She brought him provisions as a token of fidelity and thanks."

Pio: "The memory of Josiane hadn't surfaced in my thoughts, which were too jumbled by my release and new life. But a few days after I got home, I happened to meet her when I visited the home of Édouard Twagirimana, a farmer who'd been in jail with me in Rilima. Josiane was with Édouard's niece, named Mukandekezi. We surprised each other, greeted each other with joy, pouring out words of good feeling. After two weeks, she came by my land to say hello to me, encouraged by the neighbor woman, Mukandekezi. Her presence affected me strongly. It was most extraordinary to see a woman survivor visit a released killer at his house, without lending an ear to vicious gossip. Reason why I appreciated and loved her so much.

"After two visits, I made inquiries to learn what kind of worker she was. I was quite reassured. I decided to propose marriage to her. A soldier from Kanzenze, a Tutsi, had already asked her, but Josiane sent him away."

Fifi: "Clearly it delighted Josiane to hear Pio had been released. Since he could not walk about freely at first, she had her friend Mukandekezi go with her to enter his yard on a visit. It was during that visit that Pio and Josiane agreed on the plan for marriage, perhaps to express their gratitude on both sides: Pio, for her gift of provisions in Rilima; Josiane, for being spared in the marshes. But maybe they'd already come to an agreement, long before, in that hiding place."

Pio: "The engagement was arranged without complications. The two families agreed on the date and the drinks. A man named Mwumvaneza promised me the cow for the dowry. But when he refused to give it on the last day because of the fiancée's ethnic group, I was obliged to borrow it from Kayinamura, the man in charge of my wedding party, on condition that I give it back to him after the ceremony. The agreement was indeed accepted by both sides.

"We brought a case of Primus, one of Mutzig, two jerry cans of *urwagwa*, and seven of *ikigage*, the sorghum beer, to Josiane's family house. I paid for everything, since the family refused to participate. On my side I had a single Hilux van. Many guests set out on foot—not a big problem as they were used to walking.

"On Josiane's side, they were well prepared, too, with a van to transport the distinguished guests. We reached the church at three o'clock, late enough so that I was fined five thousand francs. That day ended without incident, both families distrustfully refusing to split the traditional purchase of wedding drinks and household utensils for a newlywed couple's home."

Fifi: "When Josiane announced her marriage, her family set up an outcry of opposition. The relatives said, 'We can't marry you to one of those who murdered your father and brother!' They kept saying that if she got married, she'd have neither assistance nor dowry. They promised she'd be driven out, warned her she'd be cursed. But the girl never gave in. She answered, 'Your curses don't matter—you say he has a reputation as an *interahamwe*, but no suitable Tutsi on the hill has asked for my hand. I'm not a little girl anymore. I'd rather take the one who saved my life than those who shun me.'

"Afraid of the scandal of an illegal marriage, the mama finally consented. Besides, she knew no more suitors would show up at the house after the rumors about that secret relationship, and her daughter was getting on. In the end, though, Josiane had real help only from her maternal aunt, who's doing well in Kigali. She's actually the one who rented the van and bought the drinks. She preferred to pay for everything at the last moment, to avoid covering the family in shame.

"Anyway, Pio's family put up a more vigorous fight, especially the mama and sisters. They shouted, 'A Tutsi woman is lazy, useless for farming, she keeps her hands soft, she'll be here only to share the land! She'll eat, and defy us. She can spy on us and betray us at any moment!' The mama even threatened to accuse her son about the killings during the *gaçaças*, to send him back to the penitentiary and break up his union with Josiane. But Pio paid them no attention and began making the adobe bricks for his new house.

"So the engagement was made against the will of both families. As a colleague of Josiane's older brother, I accepted an invitation to the wedding. There were several outbursts of words to show for everything, and nasty things were said from camp to camp, but that was all. The families gave nothing in the way of household items. Pio dowered Josiane with a borrowed cow. The two sides were very much at odds. Few people accompanied Josiane to Pio's house, many preferring to go guzzle fresh libations in the *cabarets* of Nyarunazi."

Pio: "After the wedding, everything took a wrong turn. The family's hatred showed its face over the property. It was in fact my sister Catherine, the widow of an *interahamwe* killed by the Patriotic Front in 1994, who started the muttering and insults about Josiane. Then my mama tried to confiscate the place where I was building the house. That plot, I'd received it directly from my father on his deathbed, a thing well known to everyone in Nyarunazi. Awful threats were made toward Josiane to scare her and send her back home.

"On October 10, 2005, the situation became serious. In the early morning my mama came to attack my house, armed with a sharpened machete. I went outside with mine. I pushed my mama, she fell on her back, she hollered for help. Since no one came running, she got back up and cut four stems of bananas from meanness. She was trying to goad me, make me commit a fatal mistake. She was provoking me so I would return to prison and Josiane would get chased out. But Josiane stayed calm, she grabbed my arm, held me back from the edge of the trap. She brushed off the spiteful words and went on down into the field. Since that day I keep an eye out so my wife will not be abused by these venomous people, and I wait for them to accept the truth about my inheritance and my marriage."

Fifi: "The mama and Pio each complained to the local court about the quarrel and the inheritance. Around the time of the *gaçaça*, the mama tried to stir up revenge on the hill, wanting to push her son into a second condemnation for the killings. But she grew wary and stopped, because the business had reached the irritated ears of the authorities.

"Josiane will not be driven from the land, she's stubborn. She busies herself with the house or goes to the field. She has gotten used to farming. She behaves very nicely to her Hutu neighbors. She's cheerful, she makes jokes, she's already laughing at everything like a Hutu woman. Pio and Josiane went to pay court to Josiane's family. Josiane's teacher brother is getting somewhat used to Pio, they've had drinks together. But Josiane's family never visits Pio's mother, fearing the shame of seeing themselves denied the traditional presents."

Pio: "I haven't kept a single harmful scar from the killings. I learned to accept what happened in the marshes. I have become a better person than before, with the same character. I had been dragged into an unknown evil, I was punished in prison, I learned to avoid squabbles with survivors. I mix with people without any hidden thoughts, I push away the desire for vengeance. Josiane will conceive our first child; I feel impatient for my new family. I no longer own the entire banana plantation because of the inheritance disputes; my land has shrunk but it's fertile; it also provides beans and sweet potatoes in abundance. If drought gives us a breather, we can sell *urwagwa* twice a month. Josiane is a seamstress but she's adjusting nicely to farming. Together we will bring in satisfying harvests."

Fifi: "What did they say to each other, hiding in that hut? What promises were made? They'll never tell. It would be too shameful. And too dangerous. For Josiane, having been saved like that while her papa and brothers were cut down in the marshes. For Pio, having deceived the gang and taken part in so many expeditions. A schoolchild's love touched them; the marshes brought them together; afterward, acknowledgment or gratitude reunited them; now they are bound by a terribly secret love."

A POLICY OF RECONCILIATION

Houses burned down, sheet-metal roofs carried off, straying livestock, streets clotted with corpses, doors banging in the wind, mounds of debris . . . Summer 1994: the desolation pervading Nyamata was so appalling that journalists who passed through at the time were not able to recognize the town ten years later, during the commemoration events. The destruction left by the Hutu exodus was like the aftermath of a war, and it created a haunting impression of sudden abandonment that had not been dispelled by the deployment, on May 14, of a regiment of *inkotanyi* from the Patriotic Front.

Those troops had fanned out along the edge of the marshes, helping to lead around 2,500 people from the killing grounds. The atmosphere was described by Francine Niyitegeka: "When the *inkotanyi* saw us finally creep out like mud beggars, they were stunned as we passed by. Most of all, they seemed bewildered, as though they were wondering if we were actually still human after all that time in the marsh. Our gauntness and stench disturbed them. It was a disgusting situation, but they tried to show us the utmost respect . . . They were clearly having trouble believing all this. They wanted to appear sympathetic, but they hardly dared whisper to us, as though we could no longer truly understand reality. Except, of course, for some gentle words of encouragement."

Most of the survivors were escorted to encampments at the end of Nyamata's main street; others scattered quickly into the fields, finding shelter and sometimes goods and provisions in abandoned houses, as Innocent Rwililiza remembers: "Myself, I was sleeping in a small house, living without any assistance, waiting for sundown to go try scrounging a bottle. Fate did not treat all the survivors in the same way, however. Some found relatives or a job. An enterprising few still had a small reservoir of strength for foraging; a lucky hand might turn up sacks of grain, buried motorcycles, wandering cows, even caches of money. The hurried confusion of the Hutu fugitives enriched them, so to speak."

Those fugitives marched toward Congo in a massive procession of fifty thousand men, women, and children who had themselves already looted the fields and houses of the fifty thousand Tutsis slaughtered by machete.

During that same summer, Tutsi exiles from Burundi and Tanzania showed up in Nyamata. Their noisy arrival by bus transformed the atmosphere of desolation. They sang, honked horns, and waved banners like soccer fans. Happy to come home to their native region after years of exile, they were dumbfounded by the magnitude of the calamity before them. Most of them supported the Patriotic Front, and they stepped right into the vacant positions of authority: in the city hall, courthouse, military governorship, police station, both secondary schools, the hospital, churches, and the big *cabaret* across from the marketplace.

The hills did not lose their ghostly appearance until two years later, however, when those fifty thousand Hutus returned from Congo in columns flanked by soldiers, who quickly delivered more than seven thousand of them to Rilima penitentiary, releasing the others to face their fallow and overgrown fields, the

sword of Damocles hanging over their heads, and the Tutsi survivors with whom they would once again be neighbors.

What a destiny, worthy of Dante, for these survivors con-
demned to live with the killers and their families! How cruel
history can be! And so we see all those reconciliation plans stub-
bornly trotted out by the Patriotic Front in power, the American and European donors, the humanitarian organizations, the
churches, and the UN institutions sitting at Rwanda's bedside.
But what has come of their efforts? How are they doing, these
more or less praiseworthy—or cynical—five-year plans and grand
projects for "reconciliation" (a concept with many interpreta-
tions)? How is it going, this political, psychoanalytical, liturgical
reconciliation?

Let's imagine a foreigner arriving in Nyamata today, where a
guide awaits him. He moves into a room in the parish complex
managed by a Hutu priest or one at the new hotel opened by
Émmanuel, a Tutsi. He strolls around the marketplace; he goes to
Mass, where he's thrilled by the singing. At the soccer field,
standing by the spectator rail among the merry onlookers, he
watches the Bugesera Sport team, which outclasses Kigali's classy
clubs in the first division. The next day, he invites himself to tour
a primary school. Everywhere, his guide shows him Tutsis and
Hutus side by side and assures him there are no clashes between
the two groups. The foreigner may request an audience with the
mayor, then an interview with the official in charge of the *gaçaças*,
and talk at length with a secondary-school teacher: they will all
describe the serious tone at town meetings, court sessions without incident, the studious atmosphere in school. In short, an
ongoing reconciliation.

That illusion will last for two or three days before the first
unmistakable cracks appear in its facade. As the faithful leave after

Mass, for example, they divide into two groups at opposite ends of the church courtyard to discuss the sermon and the week's news before going on home, without a word having passed between the two communities. At the marketplace, farm women exchange dark looks and won't speak to one another. At the *cabaret* frequented by the town veterinarians or the one favored by truck and taxi drivers, one customer off by himself drinks alone or tries in vain to join the general conversation. Elsewhere, someone refuses a greeting or a proffered swig of *urwagwa* with a curt gesture.

Outside Nyamata, the farther the foreigner goes into the hills, the more these contradictory signs jump out at him. People walking along abruptly cross to the other side of the path, sneering or muttering insults at a passerby. Returning home from the market, folks wait at the entrance to the forest to walk through it in a group. I remember what Sylvie Umubyeyi told me when we first met: "There are those who fear even the hills where they should be working their lands. There are those afraid of meeting Hutus on the road. There are Hutus who saved Tutsis but who no longer dare go home to their villages, for fear that no one will believe them. There are people scared of visitors, or the night. There are innocent people whose faces inspire fear and who dread inspiring fear, as if they had the faces of criminals. There is the fear of threats, the panic of memories."

The foreigner climbs up to the town center on Kibungo Hill, where farmers come to relax for a while after the day's labors. Over here, a gathering of Tutsis deep in conversation, and over there, a hundred meters away, a group of Hutus. Your interpreter can point out exceptions wherever you go: Ignace seeking advice about his calves from Tutsi cattlemen; Fifi chatting with her Tutsi girlfriends. And yet, as soon as the foreigner begins to talk with people, he will feel a growing uneasiness, a malaise that will become a daily experience and that can change to anguish or a kind of nausea during his stay—and perhaps even after his return home.

What do the people think of this cohabitation and this leitmotif of "reconciliation"? Do they speak of it among themselves, and if so, when? Since reconciliation is the cornerstone of an imposed policy and the key word of Rwanda's foreign donors, I expect to hear boring, politically correct answers. To my astonishment, Hutus and Tutsis—those who participated in my two previous books, in any case—express themselves with an instructive freedom of sincere speech.

Ignace Rukiramacumu: "Recovering trust, intermarriage, that's done for. But sharing drinks, giving cows, helping one another out in the fields, that will depend on each person's character. Hutus can make peace more easily than Tutsis, because they become normal people again more easily. They have lost less. It's loss that damages a person deep inside and makes forgetting so hard.

"Reconciliation is an obligation for Rwandans, who have no other territories except their small country. It will be deeply painful, but it will succeed, because the authorities are being fair to both camps, by making everyone accept it equally."

Alphonse Hitiyaremye: "I'm adapting the way I should to my new life. I cleared my fields, I gave up my *cabaret* because it went bankrupt. I'll never regain my former level of wealth, but that's all right. The killers step back into life more quickly than the survivors. They accept the hard toil of the fields more readily, because they haven't abandoned their zeal along the way like the others. They clear land even right into the backwaters of the marshes when a dry spell lingers; they irrigate new plots, they stock up harvests to sell at useful prices; they distill a lot of *urwagwa* and heat up the market.

"The Tutsis—you can see they don't work as they used to. They are still desolate. They go on suffering, one way or another, and show themselves to be vulnerable. Their courage fails them if the rains skip a visit. They fall by the wayside.

"Hutus, they are reinvigorated: they thought themselves finished forever. The proof? Their wives kept having children without them! Then these men found themselves free once again. Reason why they consider the reconciliation quite profitable.

"I joined two agricultural cooperatives with the sugarcane planters along the Nyabarongo River: that's eighty-three Hutu and Tutsi farmers in all and, with the farmers growing foodstuffs, one hundred and thirty growers. We organize raffles to help with purchases, we stand one another to drinks, we talk together quite properly. But speaking in friendship, that's another matter.

"The state played its role to keep revenge from overtaking reconciliation. One cannot erase vengefulness completely from the minds of survivors. I know, I have been forgiven not by them but by the state. The survivors, even if they do their share, they don't feel safe next to the killers, they're scared of being pushed around again. Trust has been driven out of Rwanda. It will wait behind many generations.

"Me, I don't wonder why we went along with the upheaval. We were pushed by very eloquent authorities. We received orders to go down to the marshes, and then we went back there without being told to. So it's a delicate matter, today, to distinguish the harm done by each man. Going to beg pardon of one specific person, that's worthless, that's already a waste of effort.

"Personally, I think that Tutsi faces hide their reproaches

because they were strictly instructed to do so. I feel free to live from now on in good understanding and perfect security."

Pancrace Hakizamungili: "In prison, lots of killers do not accept the fact that they were defeated and that they botched the genocide. In fashionable neighborhoods of Paris or Nairobi, notorious leaders remember their lost glory with regret; they suffer only from nostalgia, and long for chaos to return them to Rwanda. They are the 'negationists.'

"If no one tampers with it, the truth never deceives. This is indeed true: many Hutus were shot by the soldiers of the Patriotic Front on the hills and later in the camps in Congo. Many Hutus were dispatched by fatal illness in prison as well. Still, their losses cannot compare to those of the Tutsis. Hutus were not cut in a program of extermination. They did not see their babies, still at the breast, slammed against walls, or the mamas cut short at the legs. It's clear today that we are not weak and traumatized like the survivors.

"The negationists blow on the embers of hatred, they spark confusion in the minds of those living together in hopes of better days. The naysayers aim to sting the survivors' nerves, and so thwart all good understanding."

Élie Mizinge: "Fear of brutalization: that's the enemy of conciliation. President Habyarimana's *akazu* let it be known that if the Tutsis reclaimed the throne, Hutus would suffer as their ancestors had under the reign of the *mwami*, that the state would force them to work without payment in money or a share in the harvest, and that they would once more see herds trampling fields without ever feeling the stick. Reason why they decided on the end of the Tutsi population. That is over.

"Now the new situation seems proper, since no one is thinking of mistreating the rival ethnic group. The survivors forget nothing of the killings and that's understandable. Myself, I was to have been shot for what I did. I shook with fear in prison; pardon accepted me. I hope to be reconciled with my neighbors."

Fulgence Bunani: "Reconciliation is a very beneficial political policy. We're quite satisfied with it. But reconciliation is fragile: if the new authorities weaken, if war with Uganda or Congo threatens Rwanda, if the Whites come back to heat up quarrels . . . And many folks remain aloof, closemouthed. They no longer sow hatred, but they are not throwing away the seeds."

. . .

What are you griping about
life is life
what did you dream about in your out-there?
Of eating your fill
of sleeping your fill
of loving your fill
Of eating sleeping loving
you have that
since you've come back.
That whole story
it's over
be happy like everyone else
that story is old history
now
is life.
And why then did you want to come back?

Leaving history behind
to enter life
just try it you lot and you'll see.

—CHARLOTTE DELBO,
The Measure of Our Days★

Marie-Louise Kagoyire: "Yes, we're enduring this cohabitation, but we're striving to rise above ourselves so as not to load another burden on a head that is already bowed down. Reconciliation? I can't give a precise definition of that word. Cohabitation is one form of reconciliation, though. Still, trust is unthinkable in the future. Sometimes I meet a stranger. I consider his bearing, his stocky figure; I observe the features of his face, and I wonder, This gentleman, for example: with what viciousness would he have killed if he'd found himself in the marshes?

"I was a lady in a prosperous family. My husband was strong and respected; his name was Léonard. I managed two shops, some fields, I really lived a good life. Then I was offered up to death: I hid in a doghouse, I escaped, I lost everything. I accept my wearisome second life, I consent to a good understanding with the Hutus, but I reject friendship. Basically, I want to defend myself so as not to favor my enemy, for if he sees weakness in me, that makes him happy. Living together in trust, like before—no one can hope for that, not even them."

Berthe Mwanankabandi: "The Hutus don't understand that we need to *know*. They are not damaged, they still have family life,

---

★ *In March 1942, Charlotte Delbo and her husband, Georges Dudach, were arrested for their activities in the French Resistance; the Gestapo shot Georges and sent Charlotte into l'univers concentrationnaire. Her masterpiece, the trilogy* Auschwitz and After (None of Us Will Return, Useless Knowledge, *and* The Measure of Our Days), *is an unflinching account, in poetry and prose of remarkable lucidity and tenderness, of her experience in Auschwitz and Ravensbrück and her return to France, where she became an important literary figure.* —Translator's note they feel well supported. They profit from the pardons and the *gaçaças*. They put a little shame on their faces only to walk the paths, and they are lying.

"Some say they've been corrected; others grind their teeth or spit out threats. Fear dogs us constantly, especially for a woman who has been raped. When I see a farmer coming up from his field, a sharpened machete on his shoulder, I must sometimes keep myself from running away. We get used to it. Everything can be learned, above all what *must* be learned, like the policy of reconciliation.

"We speak less about the past. It isn't that we've forgotten; it's time itself that has brought improvements. Still, when a drought settles in, when money goes into hiding, when food becomes scarce, fear shows up again at the door . . . When faces droop, when the earth yields nothing but problems, when there are no longer relatives to lean on, all the memories of the genocide come swarming back to plague us.

"I do not believe the next generation will be reconciled better than ours, because the children are largely blighted by what happened and by what their families say. It's too hurtful to expect a mama willingly to teach her child the required attitude. Perhaps after all the survivors have disappeared."

Angélique Mukamanzi: "The state has clamped down on our lives. And when we realize that we cannot kill one another, that we cannot squabble all the time, we choose to forget a little. Nature carries us along. The Hutus offer good behavior. The Tutsis are accommodating. Destiny returns to its path, but the war has not had its say."

Jeannette Ayinkamiye: "The authorities have decided not to add to the prisoners' suffering because, like the priests, they see no advantage in it. That amazes me, but life gives me no choice. Only the authorities can protect me. Myself, since I am too weak to punish the criminals, I've thrown my lot in with the pardon. We obey, we acquiesce sincerely. Except, obviously, when fears of drought or sickness revive memories of the killings."

Janvier Munyaneza: "Everyone can change; we can, too. It's not scandalous to change so long as we don't forget those we lost, and how they were cut down.* The Hutus' wrongdoing becomes less serious when life agrees to smile. A man who recovers his cows, who weighs up a fine harvest, or a woman who finds a husband again and watches her children grow—for them, sorrows begin to fade, and remembrance no longer burns quite so much. But for the sixty-year-old mama who no longer has children flocking around her and must fetch her own water, reconciliation . . . there's no point in saying that word in front of her."

Sylvie Umubyeyi: "Why shouldn't it be possible to reconcile? Personally, I think it's quite possible. To live in harmony as before, well, that's out of the question, but why not be eighty percent reconciled? The missing twenty percent . . . is trust. As for the other feelings—all right, they're enough to move forward.

"Before, I was too affected by fear. Whenever I saw a killer, I thought of my vanished relatives, of all I had lost. As I already told you, if we linger too long in the fear of genocide, we lose hope. We lose what we've managed to salvage of life. Myself, I still hope to be happy in the future. I don't want to keep bitterness in my heart and die from that. Someone orphaned by the

---

* Most of Janvier's family died in the massacre in the church at nearby Ntarama, where he saw his pregnant oldest sister's belly cut open "like a sack." Beaten with an iron bar, left for dead under a heap of corpses, he was rescued by his father and older brother; together they fled to the papyrus marshes. Now he has only his brother. —Translator's note

genocide with no more parents, no more family, no house anymore, no job . . . he can't imagine any reconciliation, and it's the
same for an old mama. As for me, I'm not suffering physically, I
have lovely children, I can travel, I can talk. I was cut in my life,
but I want to pursue life, absolutely. Even if I no longer trust my
neighbors, I still have confidence in myself."

Innocent Rwililiza: "I believe in reconciliation, but reconciliation
with myself first of all. On the morning when it all began, I
looked out the window and saw a neighbor step outside with his
gun. I knew he was coming after me. I fled; my wife went to the
church. We never saw each other again, and I have lived as a
guilty man. But the years have convinced me that it was chance,
nothing else, that turned me away from the path to the church.
The more reconciled one is with oneself, the more one thinks of
reconciling with others. I have remarried. My new wife has supported me in hardship. Now I have four new children, I'm
greeted warmly in the street, I'm a school principal, and my colleagues respect me: all signs of reconciliation.

"Making peace with the Hutus would mean mixed marriages,
giving cows to one another, sharing real conversations. Unimaginable. After all, they cut enough to break their own arms without a second thought. That is truly the most astounding part of
it. Thoughts such as: If I cut this much, will I solve my problem?
Won't I someday need those neighbors I left in the marshes? If I
kill like this, won't I be killed, too, in the end? No, really, the
idea that they never even wondered about anything is impossible
to get used to.

"But drawing closer to the Hutus is vital. The fact is, the Tutsis don't want a country all to themselves, they couldn't survive in
a nation without Hutus. The Hutus wielded the machete against
the Tutsis, but they wield it as well against nature. The Hutus are

farming stock, and I know they are necessary to Tutsi prosperity. Hutus are stronger, more tenacious in the fields, they get along better with the earth. They are more stalwart in bad weather, for farming is in their blood. When drought attacks the fields, they can walk five kilometers farther every morning to go plant in the moist soil of the marshlands.

"A nation of Tutsis would become pastures for herds, desolate fields, and barren marketplaces. Since Tutsis tend to try outsmarting one another, there would be bickering. Also wastelands, nomadism, famine, and the Middle Ages.

"Hutus need Tutsis because of the meat and milk, and because they are less adept than Tutsis at planning projects— except for massacre projects, obviously. But the Tutsis are more dependent on the incomparable Hutu workers.

"Tutsi survivors have no future: I say this to you speaking as one of them. In three or four decades, no one will talk about all this; those who haven't succumbed to illness will die off from old age. Their children will remain, of course, but they—what will they think of their parents' burden? Will they be willing to shoulder it in turn? The survivors have already softened their grumbling from ten years ago. Now they put up with everything, go along obediently, repeat the words of goodwill, temper their discouragement.

"The other Tutsis, from the diaspora, make sure the survivors never take revenge. They know they themselves are the clever ones. They're patient, and they don't quarrel with Hutus. This is even truer in Kigali, where there are more moderate Hutus with whom one can deal confidently. The diaspora Tutsis don't forget anything—either the terror of their flight, or the wretchedness of exile, or the massacres of their families. They are neither traitors nor ingrates. But it suits them to present the genocide as a kind of human catastrophe, a dreadful accident of history, in a way, requiring formidable efforts of cooperation to repair the damage. They invented the policy of reconciliation because more than seven out of ten Rwandans are Hutus. It's a terrible thing, after a genocide: a demographic majority that snatched up the machete.

"Reconciliation would be the sharing of trust. The politics of reconciliation, that's the equitable division of distrust."

Claudine Kayitesi: "People are living peacefully, but actually they are avoiding one another. The atmosphere is chill. Danger is watching from both camps. We can be humble and nice, we'll share, we'll cooperate as we should. But believing them is unthinkable. Reconciliation is a state policy. We fear it, we obey it, we accept it to protect ourselves against the travails of life.

"Human beings cannot abandon their nature forever. We have a painful longing to live *something*. If you are a farm woman, it's to be prosperous. If you are a mother, it's to be fruitful. If you are a wife, it's to be stylish and attractive. That's why, personally, I agree to share life on the hills with the killers. It's a choice. A somewhat necessary choice."

THE GOOD OLD DAYS

How many teachers in villages (not to mention difficult suburbs) wouldn't marvel to see the pupils of the Nelson Mandela School in Kanzenze, in the already hot morning sunshine, head for their classrooms the instant the gong sounds!

This gong—actually a tin tray hanging from a frame—occupies a place of honor in the middle of the playground, next to the flagpole. Three brick buildings border this yard. The one uphill, a little to the side, not far from Eugénie's home, houses the secondary-school classes; the primary-school building is downhill; in back are the stoves where every morning in three gigantic cauldrons the cooks prepare the noon sorghum porridge for seven hundred students; and in front sits the principal's small office.

Innocent Rwililiza arrives there each morning from Nyamata via bicycle-taxi (in the evening he will hail a passing van from the bench where he sits drinking his Primus). After setting his principal's briefcase down on his desk and speedily arranging substitutes for a few absent teachers, Innocent steps out into the courtyard thronged with students to wield the mallet. Under the stern but amused eyes of their teachers, all the children abandon their games at the sound of the gong to line up with the alacrity of Olympic sprinters in front of their classroom doors. And every child places both hands on the shoulders of the one in front, in spite of any noticeable difference in their heights caused by the recent upheaval in their lives. Gradually the laughing and whispering die down; the children now stand still. The teachers, all women, hold blackboard pointers in one hand and, with the other, caress each child's head as their pupils march singing into class.

It would be useless, though, to harbor any illusions about the radiant results of this scholastic idyll, for it has never prevented conflicts and wars among its adult graduates. Ignace and Jean-Baptiste Munyankore, Joseph-Désiré and Innocent, Pio and Berthe sat on these same benches in their day, which didn't keep the ones from hunting the others years later, machete in hand.

While lessons are recited, Innocent sniffs the sorghum porridge boiling in the cooking pots, checks on deliveries from the World Food Program, and listens to requests from parents. He himself no longer teaches, aside from the one day he spends every weekend holding classes at the university. Innocent idealizes the world of knowledge and ideas. He doesn't read any more than others do, for lack of books, but he remembers the books he has read by heart. He mail-orders French child-psychology textbooks and teaching manuals, and tends to be didactic even in the *cabaret*, where he punctuates his opinions with sweeping hand gestures that become emphatic when someone contradicts him, and even more so if he's teased about his anticlericalism.

The first time we ever met, he was standing beneath the acacia tree at the town's main intersection, correcting a page written by a friend he'd just run into. He's constantly playing the role of public writer, helping others revise their letters, and when he must write one himself, he buys the precise number of sheets of paper he needs at the stationery shop and writes his letter out in one go, without any hesitation or mistakes.

He delights in explaining things to others. During the preliminary phase of the *gaçaças* he went all over the region by motor-bike to lead training sessions, even in the tiniest hamlets of the Bugesera, in schools, and in prisons. During the electoral campaign for the post of municipal councilor of Kibungo (which he landed), he relished making speeches to country folks beneath the trees. He does fear power, however, which he never challenges, and which sometimes strikes real terror to his heart, for as he says, "The killers pass on, the Whites as well, but the authorities are always with us."

Depending on his moods and whom he meets, he patronizes every *cabaret*, from the most spartan, Fifi's place in Kibungo, to the swankest, Chez Rose in Nyamata. He doesn't say, "I'm going to drop in at the *cabaret*," but "I'm going to go stand up for myself at the *cabaret*."

He loves the respect that comes from his career in education as much as he venerates the profession itself. He never misses a chance—on the road, in the forest, or in a courtyard—to have a discussion along the way with any child he meets, whom he will lecture patiently. Impulsive, anxious, sensitive, he grows calm in contact with children, in his role as an educator. Neither the killings and turmoil nor the demands made on him since then, thanks to his now formidable reputation, have had any effect on his dedication to teaching.

Because, of course, he has always led a full life, from the very beginning.

Innocent Rwililiza: "When I was little, I helped my papa during school vacations, naturally. I could only stay for half the day, but each morning I followed him out to the fields. And it was good, farming.

"As a youngster of four or five, I'd go with my parents to keep an eye on my little brothers and sisters in their basket. I couldn't dig yet, but I watched. When I was about eleven years old, I began to swing the hoe between my parents. As a boy, I became quite good at farming, on our family land or that of our neighbors. Because they'd come to us one day, a little group of five or six, and the next, we'd all go to someone else's place. It was fun. That way we could sow a larger area all at once, and if things grew, we'd rake in better harvests. When seedtime was over, the ladies would prepare sorghum mash for beer; we'd drink, the men would chat, the children listened, it was wonderful.

"My parents came to Kibungo from Ruhengeri. They received a five-acre allotment with a little house on it from the Native Welfare Fund. Those houses of plain mud brick crumbled after a year and had to be replaced by the sheet-metal/adobe dwellings of the region. My parents grew food crops: sorghum, maize, beans, and of course green bananas, an essential item for Rwandan farmers because of *urwagwa*. And coffee, of necessity, because a Belgian law of 1905 required all farmers to plant three hundred coffee bushes on the lands bordering roads. We raised four cows, I believe.

"I went to primary school in Cyugaro. At sunrise we washed and set out with a small bag of provisions, covering about five kilometers with the children from the hill, some of whom walked ten or fifteen. We listened until four o'clock: arithmetic, French—because we learned everything in French—and religion, because being Christian was compulsory. There was a soccer ball at school, and everyone had to give it a kick at least once a year. We played homegrown games, with poles and banana-leaf balls.

"At around five in the afternoon, I had to fetch water from the marshes for the household. We'd dig a hole, strain the water through a nest of grass, and fill the jerry can. In the marshes we saw monkeys, wild pigs, tortoises, and giant pythons. My father never went hunting, because his native region, Ruhengeri, was not known for that. Mama lit the fire under the cooking pot for beans every day, sweet potatoes and manioc in season. Meat never made it to the table, except on New Year's.

"The cows gave us milk and manure, and money from their sale, if a serious need arose. When we guarded cows and goats in the bush, we'd play, make hiding places, set up swings with vines. We did judo; that was most interesting. We might also get into fights after some incident or form deep friendships, like all children. We used to pinch manioc from other people's fields and roast them in secret. We'd have a feast.

"In the evening, we'd sing, listen to stories and lullabies. If our papa had made a little money, he'd head straight for the *cabaret* and we'd reap the benefit, because then our mama would storytell. She knew lots of fables, myths that humanize animals and animalize humans, just the way yours do, I suppose, plus proverbs and counting rhymes. If our papa stayed home, he worried as all farm folk do, and he'd go to bed, and our mama would have to pay attention just to him, of course. Then old mamas would storytell, because we didn't have a radio to listen to.

"I'd get to go to Nyamata when the coffee was sold, and too bad if you missed out on Papa's departure that day, because he might well get his money from the wholesaler and buy a shirt, toy, or candies. Saturdays, when there was no school, I sometimes went with our mama to the market, to barter or to celebrate a holiday like Christmas. It was a magnificent market with thousands of people who'd come from quite far away, a much more prosperous market than now. We'd eat a fresh-baked roll and watch the cars. All my childhood memories are happy ones. We harvested enough bananas; when our papa went to uncover our local brew, the atmosphere warmed with conviviality.

"In school, I was intelligent. I was in the first rank in every subject. The children liked me, and so did the teachers. Since my papa knew I was at the head of my class, he often came by to help me along in his own way: he'd slip sweets into my hand and did his best to bring me something to eat when I'd been too rushed in the morning. Mama was nice and Papa was modest, not as countrified as others were. Compared to the other primary-school pupils, I was lucky, but later, among the secondary-school students, children of well-placed people, I wasn't much at all.

"I went to the secondary school in Rilima, then to Byumba Teachers College. I'd go to Rilima on Papa's bicycle the day school opened. At other times in the year we'd climb onto charcoal trucks or walk, our suitcases balanced on our heads. It took four hours using shortcuts through the bush. We used to see elephants, antelopes, and monkeys; I even saw a lion. I was good in all subjects, but the national university was off-limits to me, reserved for the well-to-do children of the *akazu* and the regime's big shots. A peasant's child was never supposed to go ahead of the mayor's or prefect's child. Hutu or Tutsi, the little country boy just had to stay behind the 'civilized' kid: that was a government rule often repeated on the radio. So, in spite of my grades, I could choose between only two professions: teaching, for the prestige, or agronomy, for the motorbike that came with the job.

"I discovered at a tender age what set Tutsis apart. Late at night, grown-ups would tell how they'd been driven from Ruhengeri; they spoke of toppled chiefs, assassinations, beatings, and burnings, while we listened in the shadows. We sang ballads about the *mwami*, listened to Tutsi folktales. The Tutsi stood out because of their songs and jokes, which they tossed off with particular flair, especially when alcohol was flowing. And it was the cow that made the Tutsis remarkable. They were stock breeders and they loved milk. The Hutus—they ate food of better quality, and in more quantity, because they worked harder. But as for milk, it was Tutsi.

"On the one hand, yes, we were proud to be Tutsi, because that had something to do with nobility, sobriety, a kind of haughtiness. Tutsis saw themselves as taller, more slender, more delicate of feature, with a redder skin tone—especially the girls, who always felt especially pretty even if they were fat and dark-complexioned. On the other hand, no: we felt uneasy, because we were prey for massacres, we knew we were threatened in an evil way. We had to disguise our pride to avoid aggravating the Hutus. Behaving humbly outside, proudly at home, that's our character. We felt completely superior, from having occupied the throne for four centuries, and that's what drove the boasting that we whispered among ourselves. But we remained afraid.

"Hutus and Tutsis lived as good neighbors, but basically they dreaded one another and took care not to add good feelings to the good understanding. For example, they never intermarried, never on the same hill. To find a Tutsi wife, a well-off Hutu like Jean-Baptiste Murangira had to walk more than a hundred kilometers. The two groups exchanged mutual assistance and drinks, but among themselves they chewed over bitterness and hidden schemes. They swallowed down bad words, but not suspicions.

"As a child, I had a first terrible fright the day after President Kayibanda was overthrown.* That day, fifty listeners surrounded a man with a radio that was spewing bloodcurdling threats into the air. On the opposite bank of the Akagera, we could see fires flaming up. I was nine, already on the alert like all little Tutsis, old enough so that I could never forget an instant of that horror.

"After receiving my diploma, I was hired to teach at the school in Kibungo, on my hill. I no longer had to face hard stoop

---

* *This was the coup that brought Habyarimana to power in 1973. —Translator's note*

labor in the field: I lived off a salary in education, and that was a relief. On Kibungo the houses were scattered through very fertile bush. The family of Rose, my first wife, lived near our house. Rose was one of my students before she left to study in Congo. When she returned, she was absolutely remarkable. We became friends, because we worked together and had known each other since childhood. She was a well-educated girl, quite erudite and intelligent. Her father was the school principal. And she had traveled abroad. Rose . . . I admired her, I longed for her; we fooled around, and motherhood touched her. We married quickly, before that news could run around the hill and because her papa was furious. The dowry was handed over in Kibungo, the marriage performed in the district, and the celebration held at the cultural center. The guests contributed their share; we ate, we sang.

"Rose's papa wasn't at all pleased to have me as his son-in-law. This gentleman of great reputation knew the full measure of his daughter's qualities, so rarely found on the hill. He'd made certain overtures in the region with an eye to finding a husband of high social standing for his daughter, and would have liked more than a simple teacher for a son-in-law. That was understandable. But in spite of how things had turned out, he did not behave unpleasantly to me. After all, we did share the teaching profession, and the fear of massacres; this was in 1993, a year before the genocide.

"Rose and I, we moved into a two-room house in Gatare, the teachers' neighborhood in Nyamata, because the family land was becoming too crowded. With my first paycheck, I bought the bike I used to get up to my job in Kibungo. We were eagerly looking forward to the birth of our first child and were envisioning a happy life despite the threats hanging over us. Rose and I, we loved each other so, so much. As a young man, I used to dream of her. I still dream of her, more and more often. Life shoves everything aside as it goes along, except that feeling: the memory of her overwhelms me as fiercely as it ever did. I thought it would fall down the hole of forgetfulness, but no . . . Today, it's the killings that seem to be fading, not her.

"I dream more and more frequently about us, perhaps twice a week. I see us in Kibungo, at the school, on the path through the forest. I see us again in Nyamata in our little house, and how we were so happy together."

WHAT HAVE WE BROUGHT BACK
FROM OUT THERE?

Alphonse Hitiyaremye: "When I was released, I was scared to look at a survivor. Time is giving me courage; I'm able to go up to them and I feel something more human in my regret for what I did. I'm no longer the Alphonse of before; there was a small negative change, after all. Bad times have modified my thoughts. Age took the upper hand during those years of distress. Prison has damaged my ability to concentrate.

"As I told you, we found it easier to wield the machete than to be mocked and reviled. This truth makes no sense to anyone who was not there with us, but now it sometimes eats at me.

"I killed, I was imprisoned, and fear found its mark. The fear of evil—that is with me still. But most of all I've changed economically. Losing wealth keeps my intelligence from negotiating as before; I shy away from decisions, I don't spend money quickly anymore, I no longer hire extra hands. I've lost the business courage I had before the killings. I no longer feel at ease. I miss the prosperity that has abandoned me."

Pancrace Hakizamungili: "I think I am a better Pancrace than the one before the killings, because from now on I have an idea of the person I was: I have seen myself greedy and bloodthirsty. But I am chastened. I am a man improved by the experience of those cruel things; I know that I have abandoned malice along the way.

"I was pulled into savagery with my colleagues, I obeyed terrible men of authority, I took part in the expeditions waving my machete. I've returned destitute to my land. I know the heavy consequences of my misdeeds.

"Despite everything, my personality resembles what it was. I was a good and pious boy; I have become a better and more pious boy, that's all. If I may put it this way, I have been purified by wickedness."

Fulgence Bunani: "I don't think about the expeditions, and not much about the people I killed. Most of all I think about my savage state back then. That's what often disturbs me. Men are not aware of their natural bent for cruelty. If they are nudged along by bad government, if they are afraid of soldiers, if they hear rumors, they can quickly go bad. They behave savagely without seeing themselves as savages. I was manipulated by wickedness: drinking bountifully of Primus, eating cows morning and evening, killing Tutsis for no reason. Killing without a word, save for joking about the free sex or rejoicing at our successes.

"Killing without hesitation, without even the fear of getting dirty from the mud holes or the spurting blood. Killing without considering for oneself any real questions about why we were killing, or for whom—that is haunting for anyone who did it."

Pio Mutungirehe: "No one is born bad. I was frightened by the *inkotanyi* attacks and the traditional evil-mindedness of the Tutsis. I longed for the riches to come. I was hurried along by politicians.

"In Rilima I told you: that killer, he was indeed me as to the wrong committed and the bloodshed, but he is a stranger to me in his ferocity. I recognize my offense, but not the nastiness of the person tearing through the marshes on my legs, with my machete in hand. However, without any more dodging or lying, I know that it was truly me.

"But I'm a good sort. I behaved myself on the school bench, on the soccer team, in the *cabaret*, in Rilima. I am the same man as before, I am even a better person. I married a Tutsi. All that upheaval of the genocide was of benefit to my psychology, in the end. I want to get beyond that disastrous period, and I can wait patiently to be forgiven. In any case, I will not be uneasy anymore at living in good understanding with the Tutsis."

Ignace Rukiramacumu: "Old age has attacked me, poverty has attacked me, and regrets as well. I feel somewhat attacked on all sides. Before, I was levelheaded. I could talk with confidence because worries avoided me while wealth and tranquillity embraced me. I was known for my tobacco harvests, which sold at good prices all the way to Kigali. But things have spoiled.

"Today, growing tobacco proves backbreaking; money turns away from me; my strength no longer obeys me as it did. My sons harry me to claim their due of the land; my daughters bicker with my new wife. The Hutus criticize me for what I admitted during the trials. The Tutsis can well look at me reproachfully for what I have done. I do feel that such distress and confusion burden my heart and mind."

. . . A child gave me a flower
one morning
a flower he picked
for me
he gave the flower a kiss

before giving it to me
and asked me for a kiss
a child the color of licorice
and he smiled at me
that was in Sicily
there is no wound that cannot heal
That's what I told myself
that day
sometimes I tell myself the same thing now
But I don't believe it anyway.

—CHARLOTTE DELBO,
The Measure of Our Days

Marie-Louise Kagoyire: "No, since my flight to Burundi, I have not suffered from any mental problems, except that I am now terrified by crying and banging noises. But life has deprived me of many things. I was a greatly respected lady who lacked for nothing in a huge house, and, as I told you, I hid in a Hutu neighbor's yard, in the doghouse, lying on the animal's excrement. In three days I lost all worth in my own eyes.

"Frankly, I was beaten right down. Now, however, I've thrown off humiliation, and it no longer bothers me to talk about what happened. The reputation and social position I enjoyed have gone, but the human respect I owe myself leads me back to life. Not a joyful existence, but a worthy one, from which I can draw strength to avoid showing that they wounded me.

"Thanks to cultivating courage, I can feel life picking up again. During my escape to Burundi, I believed that I had lost everything, that I would live forever after in penury, and I just didn't care: I wanted only to be surrounded by survivors from then on. I kept telling myself, Live, anywhere and anyhow, forget the poverty, as long as it's with survivors. No more husband, no more child, no more company in a big house: there it is. Well, then, the only promise I'll make myself is to be a mama to child survivors from now on.

"Promise kept. You see them in my house, making progress: Mimi, Jean-Paul, and the little band. When I see them joking around the table, they are fine, and I'm pleased. When people I know visit me and sincerely accept anything I might offer them, I forget my troubles and feel satisfied. We chat, we catch up on one another's news, we take the time to laugh. I feel comforted. The taste for prosperity has left me, along with the worries and advantages of success. I like to share, I like living in friendship more than I used to. But happiness . . . from now on, that is too complicated."

Innocent Rwililiza: "I've changed. Two months after the killings, I stepped on a mine. I can't run anymore; fear sometimes grips me in my own home. During the genocide, my every-man-for-himself defense was to race flat out all day long like the antelope, and now I can't deal with that threat. Obviously, a second genocide is inconceivable in Rwanda. *Obviously*, *inconceivable*—what do these words mean in Africa? Naturally, I agonize over this.

"The memory of having been hunted doesn't bother me. When we talk with foreigners who try to understand a genocide, we have no trouble describing shameful situations as a matter of course. Actually, at the time I wasn't ashamed of anything. Many of our companions died of outrage, especially the old mamas who refused to run with their *pagnes* lifted up around their bellies, or the old papas who refused to debase themselves by grubbing for manioc on all fours.

"Me, no, not at all. Life was handing me the fate of a game animal; up to me to take it or leave it. Besides, it was the same for everyone: we all looked too much alike to be embarrassed. On

Kayumba we zigzagged, we spent all our strength racing to save ourselves and saved none of it to wonder about humiliations. We knew we would all die, but we kept on fleeing.

"Only afterward did I feel ashamed, when I left the forest to return to society: when I noticed I was being watched by children who had known me as a respectable teacher, while I climbed trees to tear off bananas or gobbled sweet potatoes with my bare hands or crouched all of a sudden to lap up water from puddles in front of passersby. I'd kept the obsessive habits of life up there: not washing my clothes, sleeping wherever I liked. I felt ashamed, yet couldn't conceal these manias. I fled to Kigali, where I immediately stepped on a roadside mine. Then, yes, I saw myself as ruined, plain fucked. I felt betrayed on all sides, just worthless, in a way.

"Life was too hateful to me, really; I was sorry I'd run so long and hard to escape the machetes. I spent four years in solitude, living alone without even a *boyeste* to fix my meals. In the morning I'd wait for the evening bottle; I'd drink without sharing. I did my own laundry on Saturday: three pairs of trousers and three shirts, scrubbed by hand. I was in shock; I thought of nothing, no longer felt sorry for myself. Girls would take pity and offer to help; I thought they were making fun of me. Some colleagues tried to comfort me, but I kept aloof. Basically, I thought I was degraded and abandoned, but that wasn't true.

"Today, however, another and more treacherous humiliation has come to the fore. When I see Hutu families doing well, when I see killers buckling down to the daunting work of clearing the land and gathering in harvests, when I see Hutus applying for good jobs or to study in college, or dressed up on Sundays, in elegant wedding processions—I wonder, Why do we, who ran so hard, find ourselves falling behind as also-rans? With our psychological problems, our meager crops, and our losses? Why do we, who proved each morning how faithful we were to life, to the point of collapsing each evening from exhaustion, receive the smallest share of gratitude? Why is robust strength waiting so long to knock on our doors? Those are questions that humiliate my deepest being.

"I have recovered some of my confidence. I run a school, my new wife gives me children, some people offer me a Primus over which to discuss projects, others invite me to marriages, and I have received three cows as gifts. But I have gained nothing intellectually. Living through that genocide has brought me nothing intellectually, no enriching knowledge about universality and so on. What I have doubtless gained is a bit of hatred, if I may say so. Once I thought Hutus were just like Tutsis. Not anymore . . . To tell the truth, I find it hard to say out loud just how I see that truth.

"Yes, actually . . . one little thing: I have acquired what I call varied opinions and suspicions about each and every person. On the one hand, you believe you are great friends with someone, with whom you speak as brothers and exchange cows, and at the last minute he chases you with his machete. On the other hand, you see yourself ill-used, in the depths of abandonment, and a woman agrees to marry you even though she knows you've been stripped of everything, including courage. She straightens you up and brings you home when you're unlucky, broke, and lashing out. This is a lesson: a person's importance is invisible, as is the disappointment or satisfaction this person will bring you in the end.

"As for me, good luck has touched me. I saved my life; my new wife, Épiphanie, backs me up very well, as I said. I'm holding my own in Nyamata, where I mix with important people without fear. My position is becoming respectable. I'm no longer neurotic, like the little Tutsi teacher I once was, who would have ended his life drinking *urwagwa* after work with farmers and never ever leaving his hill.

"Still and all, my character truly has been broken. I'm less merry, less tenacious, less easygoing. I make more and more blunders, step out of line more often. I have lost control over my good and bad sides. I've begun to take up small projects with enthusiasm again, but drop them without a second thought. I live on my little island from day to day. I constantly neglect my appearance and have lost that sense of how to behave appropriately in any circumstance. When people point this out to me, I reply, 'Why should I care about keeping up a facade? That doesn't matter one bit to me anymore.'

"I brought back some habits from Kayumba, and some resolutions, too, many of which I've respected, such as never again setting foot inside a church, and others I've abandoned. Not speaking to Hutus anymore, for example.

"I also returned with quite a keen sense of curiosity. Before, whenever we discussed rumors that a genocide was in the works, we never believed them, thinking that out in the countryside our lives were too deeply rooted for any change. We could believe in a few catastrophes, but not in such utter chaos. That previous naïveté now tears at my heart.

"Having lived through the killings, I have revised my theories. Philosophical thoughts don't in the least sway me as they once did: I distrust time-honored ideas, no longer respect logic as I ought to. I have learned to accept the unbelievable, to be ready for anything, to think on the alert. Behind every thought, I expect betrayal. No explanation satisfies me. Suspicion stimulates my curiosity. I always want to know what's going on behind what's going on."

. . .

Engelbert Munyambonwa: "Before, I loved reading, newspapers, amusements, Ping-Pong. Not soccer but Ping-Pong. I played it very well, like an ace. As for girls, I loved them now and then. I was also quite fond of nice clothes. I'd look at myself and think, You are *it*! I was happy. All that is very far away.

"I was an engineer in Kigali, and in Douala I was a project manager, I drew up plans. Afterward I returned home, near Kayenzi. I lived with my parents and younger sister; my brothers had office jobs in town. We had almost everything. Cows, fruit trees—you can still see them, around the house, and a fine palm grove. Life, oh, it was good. No poverty. We were content.

"Before, I didn't drink much. These days, I drink because I have nothing to do. After the genocide, my psychology was changed, and now I can't help myself. My brothers and sisters were massacred. In the foliage of the marshes, I saw myself dying like an animal. Humiliated? No, I did not feel humiliated, I was too panicked: like many others I had a dreadful fear of the machete. I found myself eating things raw, sleeping in the mire; I couldn't manage to pray anymore and thought, So what? I just didn't want to be cut. Chance gave me a lucky break.

"Still, I can say that ever since we were rescued, I haven't been in good shape. I lost my family, have no wife, no children, and the land around here is fallow or worked by strangers. I watch human forms pass by as if they were ghosts. I find myself quite alone. I tried to plow the field, but it's a good five acres, with the drought, and no wife to help me. I quit. I was forced to stop farming.

"Now nothing suits me. I'm fifty-nine, I have no more money, job, or decent reputation. I even sold some trees and sheet-metal roofing to buy drink. I think I'm too lonely. I can't find anything to cling to. I sleep wherever I am, sometimes out under the stars. Good luck detours around me. I escaped the machetes, I wake up alive every morning, feeling manly vigor still coursing through my veins, and I know the classics, and geometry, and yet . . . I'm growing more and more downhearted. What's wrong? Nothing pleases me. As soon as I start, I stop. I'm strong but can't find the strength to finish the slightest little project. I avoid people who reproach me, flee those who remind me of who I once was; I push away advice, fear scolding and sneers. I don't want to be bothered anymore. I sneak through each day, except when I meet up with someone who understands me, with whom I can drink and talk without being jeered at.

"I rise at five every morning, a habit from childhood when before going off to school I had to drive the cows down to the marshes to drink. Now I can't sleep later than five even though I have nothing to do. I'm afraid of dreams. I get up and go out. Backbiters say I'm up so early to get a free taste of the *urwagwa* just finishing its distillation for the coming day. That's foolishness. At five I'm not drinking yet, but I walk around, thinking about all that before I do drink."

Sylvie Umubyeyi: "I had everything, so I wasn't expecting anything, and I lost it all. My family, their affection, their support, my friends, my possessions, my job. For a time I also lost my taste for life. Then I found hope again. Courage came back, and with it that zest for living. I love music, I eat well, I sleep the way I always did, I can afford to wear pretty clothes. I like strolling around, talking with people, meeting friends. My high spirits deserted me during my escape to Burundi; they've returned, and I'm back in good form. My life is full of difficulties and expectations, and I know that I can find people to help me, solutions for all my petty problems. I wait. I am quite calm. Since I am alive, I cannot get tired of living; how could I? Happiness, why not: to be one day at peace with myself."

. . .

Berthe Mwanankabandi: "In the marshes we lived like pigs, a life that left its mark on us. Obviously, we're not going to do it again, but we know we really did go through that. We no longer look the same way at that animal life. We've kept certain habits, for example: not properly filtering drinking water anymore, not paying as much attention to the cooking, eating quickly, or eating where neighbors can see us.

"Time clears up those loose ends; I don't feel nearly so negligent anymore. Still, memories depend as well on the life we lead. If we are struggling, if we despair over loneliness and drought, we feel more like survivors, like people saved from a disaster. If the harvest is abundant and we needn't worry so much about the future, we feel more restored, more alive.

"In the marshes, the killers taunted us insultingly; but since there were so many of us hiding in the papyrus, we didn't feel personally humiliated. We knew the threats were the real danger, so we paid the insults no mind. In fact, I no longer feel shamed by that filthy life, except when I hear killers laugh at us and revisionists tell their lies.

"Personally, I was extraordinarily lucky not to have been raped, so I don't have to feel ashamed about that. The deep malaise, though, is something else: I feel it always, and the loneliness that comes with it. I don't recognize the girl I was before the killings; when they were over, I found myself all alone, surrounded solely by despair. I thought myself the only one to feel lonely. I believed that only I could understand what I was going through. I couldn't find kind company even among the survivors, among the good friends who'd shared that evil fate with me. My sole friend had become my sad self.

"Before, like all Rwandan children, I used to think about good and evil. I believed in honorable effort, decent behavior, the strait and narrow path. In the marshes I learned that any belief can vanish on a first morning of machetes: virtue, for example, and its rewards, the attendant or well-deserved advantages and joys. From now on I'm suspicious of moral maxims, of worthy lessons and respectable words.

"I know that those killings are unparalleled; unfamiliar with history, I cannot measure their gravity. And they have changed me. I don't know what else I can say to you since your last visit. What fresh replies do I have to all these new questions you have about the killings? Their memory does not upset me as much. I no longer shelter myself every day in fear. I don't keep away from the human beings around me anymore. Nonetheless, I do think these memories are dangerous. My former existence stopped dead. It has started up again in a new direction. All the things I expected in my first life—I can't find them anymore in my second one.

"My parents were raising ten cows; they tended a flourishing banana grove and had to spread their money out on the table to count it when they came home from market. With eleven children, and apprentices for the harder chores, we formed a considerable family. We listened to plays and music on the radio, and we kids could have sleepovers in the homes of prosperous neighbors. I was spoiled. I was a top pupil in primary school, and my parents intended to pay the fees for secondary school. I would have finished my humanities, studied in Gitarama or even Kigali, and I'd be a well-to-do woman like so many others.

"Nowadays I rise with the dawn to fertilize the soil and feed the children . . . and my thoughts cloud over. My innermost self is prey to hatred, and fear; I can be carried away by aggression and left stranded by joy. Accepting a husband, living a happy family life—I don't see that.

"I'm not looking to marry, that's the real reason I have no

suitors. For an orphaned survivor, choosing the right husband is a nightmare. If he has no problems and doesn't understand you, that won't work; if he understands you but has too many problems himself, that's no better. If he fears your problems will sabotage a perfect wife, he backs off. Reproaches can hem you in on all sides. In Rwanda it's the families that make peace between a bickering husband and wife. It's risky to give yourself on your own to a husband, without relatives with whom to take refuge, without a mama's shoulder to cry on. I'm too impulsive; I've endured too much to risk not being comforted by a husband when I become inconsolable. I prefer the anguish of a woman alone, giving birth to children on the side, of course, because that—no woman can give that up.

"In the marshes, we told ourselves that if we were lucky and were spared, we wouldn't sell off chickens anymore but enjoy them ourselves. We didn't keep our word, because tender chicken meat—well, we couldn't care less. Myself, I loved ripe bananas, and I have lost my taste for them. I listen to the radio without lending an eager ear to the music or theater programs. We also promised ourselves that if we survived, we would throw ourselves full tilt into every endeavor from then on—what I mean is, without holding back for no good reason. And that was the first promise forgotten."

Francine Niyitegeka: "My fiancé, Théophile, married me without a backward glance. I have given birth again, to lovely children. With age, the scars are fading on my skin. The herd is fattening on the lush grass along the riverbank. Tranquillity offers good understanding among the neighbors of the *mudugudu*. Time is kind to me. But although I am relieved, I am never at peace.

"Deep down, I, too, feel oppressed by walking behind the fate that was set for me. Someone who saw herself in muddy detail as a corpse in the papyrus lying among all the others, comparing herself to all those dead, always feels distressed. By what? I cannot say; I don't know how to express it even to myself. If her spirit has accepted her end, if she has at some point understood that she will not survive, such a person has seen an emptiness in her heart of hearts that she will not forget. The truth is, if she has lost her soul even for a moment, then it's a tricky thing for her to find a life again."

CHRONOLOGY OF EVENTS IN RWANDA
AND ESPECIALLY IN NYAMATA

1921 Rwanda and Burundi, formerly part of German East Africa and occupied by Belgian troops during the First World War, become Belgian territory under a League of Nations mandate.

1931 Identity cards specifying the ethnic group of the bearer are introduced, a policy continued until 1994.

1946 Rwanda becomes a UN trust territory administered as a Belgian colony and part of Congo.

1959 The last great Tutsi king, Mutara Rudahigwa, dies under mysterious circumstances. Subsequent Hutu peasant revolts and massacres cause the exodus of hundreds of thousands of Tutsis. In Nyamata, government trucks haul Tutsis fleeing pogroms in the city of Ruhengeri to the banks of the Nyabarongo River.

1960 The Belgian Congo becomes independent, and Rwanda becomes a republic.

1961 Hutu political parties win victories in Rwanda's first legislative elections.

1962 Rwanda becomes an independent republic.

1963 In Nyamata, the Rwandan army carries out widespread massacres of Tutsis.

1973 Major Juvénal Habyarimana, a Hutu, leads a military coup d'état against Rwanda's first president (a Hutu). Many Hutus fleeing poverty and drought settle in Nyamata, where massacres repeatedly occur.

1978 Habyarimana is elected president, a post he retains until his death in 1994.

1990 The Tutsi-led Rwandan Patriotic Front, assembled in 1988 from Tutsi militias (*inkotanyi*, "The Invincibles") operating out of Tanzania, Uganda, Burundi, and Zaire, wins military victories against Habyarimana's dictatorship. The Habyarimana clan organizes Hutu extremist militias (*interahamwe*, "Those Who Attack Together"); trained by the Rwandan army and in some cases by French soldiers, the *interahamwe* later recruit the hundreds of thousands of genocidal killers.

1993 Habyarimana's regime and the RPF sign a peace agreement in Arusha, Tanzania.

NOVEMBER. A UN Assistance Mission in Rwanda (UNAMIR) is dispatched to supervise implementation of the Arusha Peace Agreement. Despite desperate pleas for additional troops from its commanding officer, Lieutenant General Roméo Dallaire, a Canadian, its initial force of 2,500 men drops to 450 men by April 14, 1994, a week after the start of the genocide.

1994

APRIL 6, 8 P.M. Habyarimana is assassinated when a missile brings down his plane as it approaches the airport of Kigali, Rwanda's capital. The circumstances and perpetrators of this action are still in dispute.

APRIL 7, EARLY MORNING. Assassinations begin of democratic figures who did not fully support Habyarimana; the victims include Prime Minister Agathe Uwilingiyimana, a Hutu. RPF forces drive toward Kigali, where *interahamwe* militias have started slaughtering Tutsis and moderate Hutus. The genocide of Tutsis begins; it will continue for about a hundred days. On the hills of Nyamata, small-scale violence completely divides the two ethnic communities.

APRIL 9. In Nyamata, *interahamwe* troops launch raids to loot and burn houses abandoned by Tutsis and to murder noncompliant Hutus; without receiving specific orders, local farmers help them.

APRIL 11. After waiting four days for directions from the government, Hutu soldiers from a base at Gako, backed up by *interahamwe*, begin systematic killings in the streets of Nyamata. On the hills, the local authorities and *interahamwe* assemble the farmers and begin their planned attacks on Tutsis.

APRIL 14–15. About five thousand Tutsis are massacred by machete in the church in Nyamata.

APRIL 15. Some five thousand refugees are massacred in the church in Ntarama.

APRIL 16. Organized hunts begin in the marshes of Nyamwiza and Kayumba Forest, where Tutsis have sought refuge.

MAY 12. Sounds of gunfire are heard from advancing RPF forces. Tens of thousands of Hutu families start fleeing toward Congo on the Gitarama road. The genocide in Nyamata commune is over.

MAY 14. RPF troops reach Nyamata and seek out survivors in the marshes. Fifty thousand corpses lie rotting in the churches, the marshes, and Kayumba Forest.

JUNE 22–AUGUST 21. After the massacres are over and before its own forces can arrive, the UN instructs the French Army to secure a neutral zone in northwestern Rwanda. This ambiguous mission (to protect the people of Rwanda? to open an escape hatch for the leaders and militias of the genocidal Hutu regime?), known as Operation Turquoise, is still the subject of fierce debate.

JULY 4. Central Kigali falls to the RPF, which installs a new government with a Hutu president and the RPF's General Paul Kagame as minister of defense. (The RPF is eventually reorganized into the regular Rwandan army.)

JULY 15. Half a million Hutu refugees begin to cross into Congo; eventually some two million Hutus fill the refugee camps of eastern Congo.

AUGUST. A new UN mission, UNAMIR II, arrives.

OCTOBER 3. The UN Security Council endorses a report describing the massacres committed in Rwanda as a genocide.

1996

NOVEMBER. Rebels opposing Congo President Mobutu Sese Seko, supported by RPF forces, invade eastern Congo; some two million Hutu refugees eventually return to Rwanda. Most *interahamwe* either are killed during this Rwandan offensive or join the return and give themselves up to the Rwandan government, but some stay in Congo, forming bands of looters or mercenaries, mostly in the Kivu region along the border.

1997

MAY 17. Rwandan army troops sweep through Congo, driving out Mobutu and bringing Laurent-Désiré Kabila to power.

2001

MARCH. The Rwandan government, faced with the collapse of its judiciary due to the death, flight, or complicity of many judges during the genocide, decrees the establishment of traditional tribal courts, *gaçaças*, both to speed up the trials of persons suspected of participating in the genocide and to involve Rwandan citizens in the collective work of assigning and admitting individual responsibility for the massacre.

2002

JANUARY 1. President Paul Kagame, strongman of the RPF, consolidates his regime and proclaims Rwanda's Third Republic.

AUGUST. *Gaçaça* courts begin to operate in Nyamata.

2003

JANUARY 1. A presidential decree concerning people convicted of crimes of genocide authorizes the conditional release of second- and third-category detainees (lower-echelon killers and their accomplices) whose confessions have been accepted and who have already served at least half their prison sentences.

MAY 5. In Nyamata, most of the members of the Kibungo Hill gang, released from the penitentiary in Rilima and sent to a re-education camp in Bicumbi, return to their homes.

2006 A commission of inquiry in Kigali examines France's conduct during the genocide. In response, the results of the French judge Jean-Louis Bruguière's investigation of Habyarimana's assassination are published on November 17,[*] targeting the entourage of President Kagame through nine indictments, including that of James Kabarebe, chief of the Rwandan Defense Forces' general staff.

---

[*] *Well known for his campaign against prostitution in the 1970s, Bruguière became France's chief investigating magistrate in charge of counterterrorism, in which capacity he tracked down and captured an aging Carlos the Jackal. He was criticized for this controversial report on the assassination of President Habyarimana, in which he claimed that Kagame had his predecessor killed to provoke the Tutsi genocide and his own accession to power. Bruguière left the bench in March 2007 in order to support the candidacy of Nicolas Sarkozy for the French presidency.—Translator's note*

2008

AUGUST 5–7. The Rwandan government issues a report prepared by a team of investigators from the Ministry of Justice, accusing thirteen senior French officials, including former president François Mitterand and former prime minister Dominique de Villepin, of giving, during the genocide of 1994, political, military, diplomatic, and logistical support to Rwanda's extremist regime and the Hutu forces that, under its direction, slaughtered 800,000 minority Tutsis and politically moderate Hutus. The French Foreign Ministry dismisses the claims as unacceptable.

NOVEMBER. Rose Kabuye, a senior Rwandan official, is arrested in Germany on a French warrant, for being complicitous in the death of President Habyarimana in 1994; she is transferred to France and then conditionally released; the event further strains Rwanda's relations with France and the European Union.